THE SUTRA ON THE CONCENTRATION
OF SITTING MEDITATION

BDK English Tripiṭaka Series

THE SUTRA ON THE CONCENTRATION OF SITTING MEDITATION

(Taishō Volume 15, Number 614)

Translated from the Chinese of Kumārajīva

by

Nobuyoshi Yamabe
and
Fumihiko Sueki

Numata Center
for Buddhist Translation and Research
2009

First Printing, 2009
ISBN: 978-1-886439-34-4
Library of Congress Catalog Card Number: 2008935153

Published by
Numata Center for Buddhist Translation and Research
2620 Warring Street
Berkeley, California 94704

Printed in the United States of America

A Message on the Publication of the English Tripiṭaka

The Buddhist canon is said to contain eighty-four thousand different teachings. I believe that this is because the Buddha's basic approach was to prescribe a different treatment for every spiritual ailment, much as a doctor prescribes a different medicine for every medical ailment. Thus his teachings were always appropriate for the particular suffering individual and for the time at which the teaching was given, and over the ages not one of his prescriptions has failed to relieve the suffering to which it was addressed.

Ever since the Buddha's Great Demise over twenty-five hundred years ago, his message of wisdom and compassion has spread throughout the world. Yet no one has ever attempted to translate the entire Buddhist canon into English throughout the history of Japan. It is my greatest wish to see this done and to make the translations available to the many English-speaking people who have never had the opportunity to learn about the Buddha's teachings.

Of course, it would be impossible to translate all of the Buddha's eighty-four thousand teachings in a few years. I have, therefore, had one hundred thirty-nine of the scriptural texts in the prodigious Taishō edition of the Chinese Buddhist canon selected for inclusion in the First Series of this translation project.

It is in the nature of this undertaking that the results are bound to be criticized. Nonetheless, I am convinced that unless someone takes it upon himself or herself to initiate this project, it will never be done. At the same time, I hope that an improved, revised edition will appear in the future.

It is most gratifying that, thanks to the efforts of more than a hundred Buddhist scholars from the East and the West, this monumental project has finally gotten off the ground. May the rays of the Wisdom of the Compassionate One reach each and every person in the world.

NUMATA Yehan
Founder of the English
Tripiṭaka Project

August 7, 1991

Editorial Foreword

In January 1982, Dr. NUMATA Yehan, the founder of Bukkyō Dendō Kyōkai (Society for the Promotion of Buddhism), decided to begin the monumental task of translating the complete Taishō edition of the Chinese Tripiṭaka (Buddhist canon) into the English language. Under his leadership, a special preparatory committee was organized in April 1982. By July of the same year, the Translation Committee of the English Tripiṭaka was officially convened.

The initial Committee consisted of the following members: (late) HANAYAMA Shōyū (Chairperson), (late) BANDŌ Shōjun, ISHIGAMI Zennō, (late) KAMATA Shigeo, KANAOKA Shūyū, MAYEDA Sengaku, NARA Yasuaki, (late) SAYEKI Shinkō, (late) SHIOIRI Ryōtatsu, TAMARU Noriyoshi, (late) TAMURA Kwansei, URYŪZU Ryūshin, and YUYAMA Akira. Assistant members of the Committee were as follows: KANAZAWA Atsushi, WATANABE Shōgo, Rolf Giebel of New Zealand, and Rudy Smet of Belgium.

After holding planning meetings on a monthly basis, the Committee selected one hundred thirty-nine texts for the First Series of translations, an estimated one hundred printed volumes in all. The texts selected are not necessarily limited to those originally written in India but also include works written or composed in China and Japan. While the publication of the First Series proceeds, the texts for the Second Series will be selected from among the remaining works; this process will continue until all the texts, in Japanese as well as in Chinese, have been published.

Frankly speaking, it will take perhaps one hundred years or more to accomplish the English translation of the complete Chinese and Japanese texts, for they consist of thousands of works. Nevertheless, as Dr. NUMATA wished, it is the sincere hope of the Committee that this project will continue unto completion, even after all its present members have passed away.

Dr. NUMATA passed away on May 5, 1994, at the age of ninety-seven, entrusting his son, Mr. NUMATA Toshihide, with the continuation and completion of the Translation Project. The Committee also lost its able and devoted Chairperson,

Professor HANAYAMA Shōyū, on June 16, 1995, at the age of sixty-three. After these severe blows, the Committee elected me, then Vice President of Musashino Women's College, to be the Chair in October 1995. The Committee has renewed its determination to carry out the noble intention of Dr. NUMATA, under the leadership of Mr. NUMATA Toshihide.

The present members of the Committee are MAYEDA Sengaku (Chairperson), ISHIGAMI Zennō, ICHISHIMA Shōshin, KANAOKA Shūyū, NARA Yasuaki, TAMARU Noriyoshi, Kenneth K. Tanaka, URYŪZU Ryūshin, YUYAMA Akira, WATANABE Shōgo, and assistant member YONEZAWA Yoshiyasu.

The Numata Center for Buddhist Translation and Research was established in November 1984, in Berkeley, California, U.S.A., to assist in the publication of the BDK English Tripiṭaka First Series. The Publication Committee was organized at the Numata Center in December 1991. Since then the publication of all the volumes has been and will continue to be conducted under the supervision of this Committee in close cooperation with the Editorial Committee in Tokyo.

MAYEDA Sengaku
Chairperson
Editorial Committee of
the BDK English Tripiṭaka

Publisher's Foreword

On behalf of the Publication Committee, I am happy to present this contribution to the BDK English Tripiṭaka Series. The initial translation and editing of the Buddhist scripture found here were performed under the direction of the Editorial Committee in Tokyo, Japan, chaired by Professor Sengaku Mayeda, Professor Emeritus of Musashino University. The Publication Committee members then put this volume through a rigorous succession of editorial and bookmaking efforts.

Both the Editorial Committee in Tokyo and the Publication Committee in Berkeley are dedicated to the production of clear, readable English texts of the Buddhist canon. The members of both committees and associated staff work to honor the deep faith, spirit, and concern of the late Reverend Dr. Yehan Numata, who founded the BDK English Tripiṭaka Series in order to disseminate Buddhist teachings throughout the world.

The long-term goal of our project is the translation and publication of the one hundred-volume Taishō edition of the Chinese Buddhist canon, plus a few influential extracanonical Japanese Buddhist texts. The list of texts selected for the First Series of this translation project is given at the end of each volume.

As Chair of the Publication Committee, I am deeply honored to serve in the post formerly held by the late Dr. Philip B. Yampolsky, who was so good to me during his lifetime; the esteemed Dr. Kenneth K. Inada, who has had such a great impact on Buddhist studies in the United States; and the beloved late Dr. Francis H. Cook, a dear friend and colleague.

In conclusion, let me thank the members of the Publication Committee for the efforts they have undertaken in preparing this volume for publication: Senior Editor Marianne Dresser, Dr. Hudaya Kandahjaya, Dr. Eisho Nasu, Reverend Kiyoshi Yamashita, and Reverend Brian Nagata, President of the Numata Center for Buddhist Translation and Research.

John R. McRae
Chairperson
Publication Committee

Contents

Contents

Translators' Introduction

The *Zuochan sanmei jing* (*Sutra on the Concentration of Sitting Meditation*, Taishō No. 614) is a meditation manual compiled by Kumārajīva based largely on Indian sources. Some portions of the text have corresponding Indian originals, as we shall see later, but there is no single text in any Indic language that corresponds to this manual in its entirety. Nor is there a known version in any other classical languages, including Tibetan. Kumārajīva's Chinese version is the only full text of this manual available to us.

The translator Kumārajīva (350?–409?) was born in Kucha, an oasis city on the northern route of the Tarim basin (in present-day Xinjiang-Uighur Autonomous Region, China). His father was an Indian monk and his mother a Kuchean princess. At the age of seven, Kumārajīva became a novice monk, and when he was nine he went to northwest India and studied Traditional ("Hinayana") forms of Buddhism. On his way back to Kucha, he converted to Mahayana Buddhism at Kashgar under the guidance of Sūryasoma, a Mahayanist monk from Yarkand, an oasis city on the southern route of the Tarim basin. In 384, Kumārajīva was captured at Kucha by the Chinese general Lü Guang (337–399), who conquered the city by order of Fu Jian (338–385), king of the Former Qin dynasty. Fu Jian, however, was killed in 385 when Lü Guang was on his way home. Lü Guang reached Guzang (a city in present-day Gansu province) in the same year and learned about the death of his king in the following year, 386. After that, Lü Guang became independent and established his own local kingdom, the Latter Liang, in the Gansu and Xinjiang areas. Kumārajīva was detained for sixteen years in this kingdom. During this long period of detention, he seems to have learned Chinese.

When Yao Xing (366–416), the ruler of the Latter Qin, conquered the Latter Liang in 401, Kumārajīva was invited to Chang'an (present-day Xi'an), the capital of the Latter Qin.

There, under Yao Xing's patronage, Kumārajīva translated many important Mahayana sutras, such as the *Lotus Sutra* (*Saddharmapuṇḍarīka-sūtra*,

Taishō No. 262) and the *Vimalakīrti Sutra* (*Vimalakīrtinirdeśa-sūtra,* Taishō No. 475), into polished Chinese. These scriptures have been very popular and broadly influential among East Asian Buddhists to this day. He also translated several significant philosophical texts, most notably the *Treatise on the Middle* (Taishō No. 1564) and the *Treatise on the Great Perfection of Wisdom* (Taishō No. 1509), and a few Vinaya texts (though the origin of the *Treatise on the Great Perfection of Wisdom* has been questioned). These texts also exerted significant influence over subsequent developments in East Asian Buddhism.

Before Kumārajīva, Buddhism had not yet been introduced to China in any systematic fashion, so the Chinese people's grasp of Buddhism was in many ways limited. Kumārajīva introduced Mahayana thought systematically, based on his profound knowledge of both Traditional and Mahayana Buddhism. He thus significantly advanced the Chinese understanding of Buddhism. He is justifiably included among the four great translators of Buddhist texts into Chinese, along with Paramārtha, Xuanzang, and Amoghavajra.

We should note here that the first text Kumārajīva translated was this *Sutra on the Concentration of Sitting Meditation.* According to the preface to this manual, the *Guanzhong-chu chanjing xu* (*Preface to the Meditation Manual Translated in the Guanzhong Area,* T55: 65a–b) by Sengrui (dates uncertain), Kumārajīva translated it only six days after his arrival at Chang'an, upon the request of Sengrui. Thus we can see the keen demand for a clear meditation manual in China.

On the whole, the *Sutra on the Concentration of Sitting Meditation* is a lucid and well-organized manual that describes the paths for becoming an arhat, a solitary awakened one (*pratyekabuddha*), or a buddha (the respective goals of the three vehicles). However, since the exposition of the path for becoming a solitary awakened one is very brief, the bulk of this manual consists of a discussion of Traditional and Mahayanist methods of meditation practice.

In the Traditional portion, the manual first advises instructors of meditation to observe the inclinations of practitioners. Practitioners are classified into five different types: those who are primarily inclined to lust, anger, ignorance, or discursive thoughts as separate tendencies, and those who are troubled by a combination of these problems. Then an appropriate remedy is prescribed for each type: for those who are inclined to lust, meditation on the impurities of human bodies; for those who are inclined to anger, cultivation of friendliness; for those who are inclined to ignorance, observation of the twelve links of dependent origination (*pratītyasamutpāda*); for those who are inclined to discursive thoughts, mindful inhalation and exhalation; for those who are troubled by several problems, calling the Buddha to mind. By practicing these methods, practitioners attain single-mindedness and can proceed to the four stages of meditation and the four stages of formless concentration. Finally, they attain the five supernatural powers.

If practitioners seek to attain nirvana directly, they first apply mindfulness to the body, sensation, mind, and elements, and observe that they are impermanent, painful, empty, and without self. Then practitioners meditate on, and finally penetrate into, the Four Noble Truths, thereby becoming partially awakened people. They then go through the four supramundane stages and eventually become arhats.

In the Mahayanist portion, practitioners are also classified into the same five types, and the aforementioned five methods are prescribed. By following these methods, practitioners see the Mahayanist truth. They then follow the bodhisattva path and eventually attain the unsurpassable awakening of buddhas (*anuttarā samyaksaṃbodhi*).

Thus, the basic methods of practice are the same for those who seek to become arhats and those who wish to become buddhas. In the Mahayanist section, Mahayanist interpretations are given to the same methods, and the advanced stages described after the five methods are Mahayanist. The general framework of practice, however, is largely the same. This suggests that to Kumārajīva, Mahayanist meditation was not separate from Traditional forms of meditation. When interpreted in the Mahayanist way, the Traditional methods can be followed by Mahayanist practitioners also.

According to Sengrui's preface, portions of this text are based on excerpts from texts by Upagupta, Pārśva, Vasumitra, Kumāralāta, Aśvaghoṣa, Saṅgharakṣa, and Saṅghasena (see table on following pages). As we can see, Sengrui is silent about the sources of the Mahayanist portion.

It has been confirmed that passages from Aśvaghoṣa's and Saṅgharakṣa's works have indeed been incorporated into this manual precisely at the places specified by Sengrui. This indicates the reliability of his preface.

Contents	References*	Sources indicated by Sengrui
1. Arhat Path (Traditional portion)		
1.0.1 introductory verses	269c29 (p. 3)	Kumāralāta
1.0.2 temperaments of practitioners	270c28 (p. 7)	Saṅgharakṣa
1.1 meditation on the impurities	271c6 (p. 10)	Upagupta, Pārśva, Vasumitra, Kumāralāta, Aśvaghoṣa, Saṅgharakṣa, Saṅghasena
1.2 cultivation of friendliness	272b1 (p. 14)	Upagupta, Pārśva, Vasumitra, Kumāralāta, Aśvaghoṣa, Saṅgharakṣa, Saṅghasena
1.3 observation of dependent origination	272c10 (p. 16)	Upagupta, Pārśva, Vasumitra, Kumāralāta, Aśvaghoṣa, Saṅgharakṣa, Saṅghasena
1.4. mindful inhalation and exhalation	273a12 (p. 18)	Upagupta, Pārśva, Vasumitra, Kumāralāta, Aśvaghoṣa, Saṅgharakṣa, Saṅghasena; the verses on the six kinds of discursive thoughts in 1.4: Aśvaghoṣa; six stages of mindful inhalation and exhalation in 1.4: "various masters"
1.5 calling the Buddha to mind	276a6 (p. 33)	Upagupta, Pārśva, Vasumitra, Kumāralāta, Aśvaghoṣa, Saṅgharakṣa, Saṅghasena
1.6 four stages of meditation; four stages of concentration on the formless realms	277b16 (p. 43)	
1.7 five supernatural powers	278b4 (p. 47)	
1.8 those who prefer concentration and those who prefer wisdom	278b27 (p. 48)	
1.9 four applications of mindfulness	278c3 (p. 49)	
1.10 heat, summit, recognition, the supreme among the worldly elements	279b9 (p. 53)	
1.11 stream-entrant (*srotāpanna*), once-returner (*sakṛdāgāmin*), non-returner (*anāgāmin*), arhat	280a16 (p. 57)	
2. Solitary Awakened One Path	280c24 (p. 61)	

Contents	References*	Sources indicated by Sengrui
3. Buddha Path (Mahayanist portion)		
3.1 calling the Buddha to mind	281a22 (p. 62)	
3.2 meditation on the impurities	281b26 (p. 64)	
3.3 cultivation of friendliness	282a1 (p. 66)	
3.4 observation of dependent origination	282c11 (p. 70)	
3.5 mindful inhalation and exhalation	285a6 (p. 82)	
3.6 Way of Seeing, six perfections, ten stages	285a9 (p. 82)	
4. concluding verses	285c1 (p. 85)	Aśvaghoṣa

* In the page citations, the first number refers to the page, column, and line numbers of the original Chinese text in Taishō vol. 15. The page references in parentheses correspond to the English translation in this volume. In both cases, the numbers indicate only the starting points of each respective section.

Most of the authors of the first half were affiliated with the Sarvāstivāda tradition, though not all of them were faithful to the orthodox tenets of this tradition. Upagupta, according to Buddhist legends, was a master of King Aśoka and is considered in the Chinese tradition to have been one of the Sarvāstivāda masters. Pārśva is said to have been a cardinal figure at the convention at which the magnum opus of the Sarvāstivāda school, the *Abhidharma-mahāvibhāṣā* (Taishō No. 1545), was compiled. Vasumitra is one of the four major masters frequently quoted in the *Mahāvibhāṣā*. Kumāralāta was a famous master of Dārṣṭāntika, an unorthodox group of people within the Sarvāstivāda tradition. Aśvaghoṣa was a celebrated Buddhist poet and is well known for his two epics, the *Acts of the Buddha* (*Buddhacarita*) and *Nanda the Fair* (*Saundarananda*). Saṅgharakṣa was the author of an important meditation manual, known as the *Yogācārabhūmi* of Saṅgharakṣa (*Xiuxing daodi jing,* Taishō No. 606), which is considered to have been one of the precursors of the magnum opus of the Yogācāra school, also entitled *Yogācārabhūmi* (Taishō No.1579). Not much is known about Saṅghasena, but many of the other masters—Pārśva, Vasumitra, Kumāralāta, Aśvaghoṣa, and Saṅgharakṣa—were active in northwest India. Therefore, by and large the methods described in the Traditional portion of this manual were based on the meditative tradition within the Sarvāstivāda community in that area.

Kumārajīva probably based his manual on the meditation methods he learned while he was there.

On the other hand, the sources of the Mahayanist portion of this manual are not clear. This portion may well be an original contribution by Kumārajīva, based on his own understanding. In a way, the structure of this manual may reflect the personal history of Kumārajīva, who first studied Traditional Buddhism and then converted to Mahayana. Perhaps more to the point are the arguments of some scholars, who point out that the Mahayanization of Buddhist meditation, which eventually led to the compilation of the voluminous *Yogācārabhūmi,* was taking place in northwest India. It is possible that the structure of this manual thus reflects the historical development of Buddhist meditation in India.

For the Chinese, this manual provided much-needed clear guidance for meditation. The old meditation manuals translated by An Shigao (second century), the first translator of Buddhist texts into Chinese, had been influential up to and including the lifetime of Dao'an (312–385). The language of these manuals, however, was rather clumsy and not easy to understand. That probably was the reason why Sengrui, Dao'an's disciple, requested the compilation/translation of this manual as soon as Kumārajīva came to Chang'an. Kumārajīva might also have intended to answer the questions of Chinese Buddhists about the relationship between Traditional and Mahayanist practices. In any case, the *Sutra on the Concentration of Sitting Meditation* exerted significant influence on the subsequent development of Buddhist meditation in China, especially on the Tiantai tradition.

Therefore, seen from both Indian and Chinese perspectives, the *Sutra on the Concentration of Sitting Meditation* is a significant text. There is a short "commentary" on this manual, the *Zazen sanmaikyō chūshaku,* by the Japanese scholar-monk Jiun (1718–1804). However, this is merely a brief unfinished draft, and the content is a very free exposition of the text from a practical point of view. Therefore, it is not very helpful for a literal understanding the text.

To the best of the knowledge of the co-translators, there is no prior complete translation of this text into a Western language. Nobuyoshi Yamabe prepared the first draft of this translation, while the final version is the joint effort of Yamabe and Fumihiko Sueki. We thank Dr. Ken'ichi Maekawa for checking our draft against the original Chinese text. We are also deeply grateful to Prof. John R. McRae, Prof. Robert Kritzer, and Mr. Ryan Ward for many helpful comments.

Note on the Translation

We have sometimes inserted numbers that are not found in the original text into this English translation in parentheses for the sake of greater readability. Numbers not in parentheses are those found in the original text. Notes appearing in italics in parentheses are interlineal notes in the original text.

Correspondences to the *Saundarananda* are also given in parentheses, e.g., (SauN 15.64). In these references, the first and second numbers respectively refer to the canto and verse numbers.

An asterisk on the title of a text indicates that the Sanskrit title given is a reconstruction.

As discussed in the introduction, in both the Traditional and Mahayanist portions, the main point is the exposition of the five methods of meditation. In the Traditional portion, the original Chinese text gives the section title before each of these methods, but not in the Mahayanist portion. However, it is somewhat unnatural to give these titles only in the Traditional portion when the two portions have almost parallel structures. So, I have inserted section titles in the Mahayanist portion in brackets.

THE SUTRA ON THE CONCENTRATION
OF SITTING MEDITATION

Translated by

Tripiṭaka Master Kumārajīva
during the Yao Qing Period

Fascicle One

It is difficult to encounter a guide who [is willing to] teach and a listener who delights in listening [to the teaching]. That which mature people enjoy listening to but petty people dislike hearing [is the teaching].

To be pitied are sentient beings who fall onto the craggy pathways of old age and death. Uncultivated people enslaved by [the bonds of] obligation and love do not feel fear in awful places due to their ignorance.

Whether large or small, in this world no element is permanent. Nothing abides for a long time. Things appear only temporarily like lightning.

This body belongs to [the realm of] old age and death and is also subject to various diseases. A thin skin [is all that] covers up the impurities [within the body], deluding ignorant people.

Your youthful appearance is always swallowed up by the rogue of old age. It is like a flower garland that cannot be recovered once it has withered.

King Mūrdhagata[1] was meritorious enough to share a throne with Heavenly King Indra. His happy rewards [for his former good deeds] were numerous but where are they all now?

[When] this king was among heavenly and human beings, his enjoyment of desire was incomparable. Still he suffered extreme pain when he died. One should awaken one's mind with this story.

Desires are enjoyable in the beginning, but they all turn into great pain in the end. They are like enemies who are nice in the beginning but who eventually destroy one's [entire] clan.

This body is a foul vessel, always releasing filthy things from its nine apertures. It is also like having boils [that are] incurable by any medicine.

3

This bony chariot of yours is very weak, entangled [as it is] in muscles and veins, with consciousness evolving. You consider it to be a marvelous vehicle and are shamelessly attached to it.

The dead are abandoned in charnel grounds and fill the graveyards. Although [they were] objects of attachment while alive, once dead they are simply discarded.

One should always reflect as follows: One should contemplate single-mindedly and should not be disturbed. [Thus] one destroys the darkness of perverted ignorance, and holding a torch, one clearly contemplates.

If one abandons the four applications of mindfulness, there is no evil the mind does not generate. It becomes like an elephant that has been spared the goad and is never able to docilely follow the path.

Today one does this, and tomorrow one does that. One is attached [to pleasure] and does not observe suffering; thus one does not realize the arrival of the rogue of death.

People are busily concerned with taking care of their own business, and they do not hesitate to involve themselves in other people's business as well. But the rogue of death does not wait, and once he comes, there is no way to avoid him.

270b   When a thirsty deer comes to a spring, it heads for water to drink [from it]. A hunter, however, has no mercy and kills without waiting for the deer to finish drinking.[2]

Foolish people are also like this, busying themselves with various matters. Once death comes, it does not wait. Who will protect them then?

People's minds yearn for fortune and status, and the desires of the five senses are never satisfied. Not even kings of large states can avoid this calamity.

Even sages who wield arrows of spells cannot escape the King of Death. When the great elephant of impermanence stamps the earth, ants and leeches are all [crushed].

Putting aside all [common] people, even the truly awakened buddhas who have crossed over the streams of samsara do not abide eternally.

Therefore you should know that what you take pleasure in must be all abandoned soon, and you should seek nirvana single-mindedly.

Later, when one abandons the body and dies, who will know whether one will be able to encounter the Dharma Jewel again or not?

[Only once] in a very long while does the Sun of the Buddha rise and destroy the great darkness of ignorance. Emitting rays of light, he shows people the right and wrong paths.

"From where have I come? From where have I been [re]born? Where shall I achieve deliverance?" Who can answer these questions?

The Buddha, awakened and omniscient, appears in this world [only once] in a great span of time. If you are single-minded and diligent, he will destroy the bonds of your doubts.

People do not enjoy the true benefit and are attached to the wicked mind. As the chief among sentient beings, you should seek the reality of [all] elements.

Who knows which path he will follow at the time of death? It is just like a lamp in a wind that does not know when it will be blown out.

The Dharma of the supreme path is not difficult, as the Great Sage has explained concretely. The wisdom to teach and the object of wisdom do not depend on the external.

If you are diligent and always practice the path single-mindedly, before long you will attain nirvana, the supreme, eternally blissful abode.

The wise associate with good people, wholeheartedly respecting the Buddha-Dharma, and being averted from the defiled and impure body.[3]   270c Thus they can be liberated from suffering and attain deliverance.

They silently cultivate tranquility of mind seated cross-legged in the woods. Diligently examining the mind, they awaken their minds and realize the objects [of their meditations].

If one is not averted from being in worldly existence and sleeps at ease without awakening, if one does not keep in mind the impermanence of the world, and if one is not afraid of what is fearful,

Then [one's] defilements are bottomless, and the sea of samsara is boundless. The ship to cross over the [sea of] suffering has not yet been built. How can you enjoy sleep?

Therefore, be awake and do not let sleep cover up your mind. Know the right amount of the four types of offerings [you receive] and learn to be content.

You have not yet escaped any of the great fears. [Thus] you should make effort diligently. When all suffering comes, regret will be useless.

Wearing a Buddhist robe and seated under a tree, one obtains food according to the prescribed method. One should not harm oneself by being attached to [good] flavors.

When one has finished eating, one should know that there is no difference at all between good and bad flavors. Attachment leads to distress and suffering, and therefore do not develop attachment to anything.

In the world-system controlled by karma, there are no good or bad things that have not been experienced before. One has already experienced all of them [in one's previous lives], and thinking of this, one should control oneself.

If one is among animals, one eats grass and thinks it is tasty. In the hells one swallows iron balls, which are red-hot with sparks flying.

If one is among hungry ghosts (pretas), one thinks pus, vomited food, fire, excrement, saliva, and other impurities are exquisite.

If one is in a heavenly palace, a pavilion decorated with seven jewels, the deities (devas) there eat food that tastes like sudhā, and heavenly ladies are there to amuse one's mind.

Noble status, or seven types of dishes of various flavors in the human world—one has already experienced them all [in one's former lives]. Why should one be attached to them again?

In one's repeated rebirth throughout this world-system, if one is averted from experiencing painful and pleasant things, even if one has not attained nirvana, one should diligently seek for its benefit.

When a practitioner of meditation first visits a master, the master should ask him: "Do you keep pure precepts? Have you not committed serious transgressions?"

If the practitioner says that he has upheld the five classes of precepts and has not committed serious transgressions, then the master should teach him the Dharma. If the practitioner says that he has broken precepts, the master should further ask him: "Which precepts have you broken?"

271a

If the practitioner says that he has broken grave precepts, the master should say: "Just as a person whose ears and nose have been cut off does not need to look in a mirror, [you should realize that] you have to leave here at once. Diligently chant sutras and advise others to cultivate merit. You should thus prepare causes and conditions for practicing the Dharma in future lives. This life has been permanently lost, just as a dead tree cannot grow flowers, leaves, or fruits even if it is watered."

If the practitioner has broken other precepts, the master should teach him to repent properly.

If he is already pure, and if the master has attained the heavenly eye and mind-reading wisdom, he should explain the method of practicing the path according to the disease [of the practitioner].

If [the master] has not attained such supernatural abilities, he should observe the marks of the practitioner. Alternatively, [the master] asks [him] as follows: "Which of the three poisons predominates in you? Lust, anger, or ignorance?"

How can one observe the marks [of the practitioner's predominant tendency]?

The marks of a lustful person are as follows: He has a lighthearted personality and has many wives and concubines. He speaks much and believes [things] easily. His countenance is joyful and his speech easy. He has little anger and little distress. He is skilled in many things, willing to learn, and knowledgeable. He loves literature and is good at talking. He is skilled in discerning the feelings of other people and is easily frightened. His mind is attached to bedchambers and likes thin clothes. He lusts for women and is

7

attached to bedding, dress, ornaments, perfume, and flowers. His mind is mostly tender and is compassionate. He speaks beautifully and likes practicing meritorious acts. In his mind he wishes for rebirth in a heavenly realm, and he has no difficulty being among people. He discriminates between beautiful and ugly people and trusts women. The fire of lust is vehement, and he frequently changes his mind in regret. He likes ornamenting himself and looking at paintings. He is stingy with his own possessions and seeks the lucky acquisition of other people's property. He likes to associate with close friends and does not like solitary places. He is attached to his abode and follows popular trends. Easily surprised, easily afraid, his mind is like a monkey.

His view is superficial, and he is thoughtless in his actions. Once his casual action has brought about desired results, he cries in joy. His body is slender, soft, and cannot endure the suffering of coldness. He is easily blocked, easily pleased, and cannot forbear difficulties. When he obtains a little, he is greatly pleased. When he loses a little, he is greatly distressed. He betrays [his own] secrets. His body is warm and his sweat smells. The skin and hair are thin. There are many wrinkles and white spots. [When] he goes out, he keeps his nails and moustache neat, and his teeth white. He likes clean clothes. He is not devoted to learning and likes to play in green gardens. Being sentimental and covetous, his mind is attached to eternalism. He approaches virtuous masters and inquires after them.

He gladly follows the advice of others and patiently endures humiliation. When he hears of a situation, he quickly understands what has been done. He discriminates between the favorable and unfavorable and is sympathetic to people in distress. He is proud, likes to win, and cannot accept violation [from others]. He likes to practice generosity and to receive good people. When he obtains good food and drink, he shares them with other people. Not worrying about small things, his aspiration is directed at big things. His eyes are attracted to sexual desire, and he is never satisfied. He has no long-term plan but is familiar with social custom. By observing the faces of people, he discerns what is in their minds. His speech is pleasant, but his ties with friends are not strong. His hair is scarce, and he sleeps little. He does not deviate from proper demeanor while he is seated, lying down, walking, or standing. He quickly rescues people in emergency with his wealth but later regrets [doing so]. Whatever he is taught he quickly learns, but later

271b

easily forgets. He is attached to his course of action and cannot change it by himself. It is hard for him to be free from his desires. The transgressions he commits are trivial. Such are the marks of a lustful person.

The marks of a resentful person are as follows: He has much distress. He is impetuous and harbors resentment. His bodily actions and speech are rough. He can endure suffering, but he is not pleased with things he experiences. He has much grief and little pleasure. He can do great evils and has no compassion. He likes fighting. His face appears exhausted, and he looks around with a furrowed brow. He is hard to talk to, hard to please, hard to serve, and hard to receive approval from. His mind is like a wound[4] and [he] exposes the faults of others. In argument he is stubborn and difficult to persuade. He is hard to move, hard to associate with, and hard to block. If he swallows poison, he does not easily vomit it up. He does not forget what he has been taught to recite. He has many abilities and many skills; his mind is not lazy. He does things quickly. He does not talk even if he wishes something. His intentions are profound and hard to fathom.

When he receives a favor, he can repay it. He is capable of assembling people, and can humbly serve others. He cannot be discouraged and can complete any affair [he has undertaken]. He is hard to be disturbed and has little to fear. He is like a lion who cannot be subdued. He proceeds straight ahead and does not waver. Once he remembers something he does not forget. He reflects and ponders on it well; he recites it [repeatedly] and keeps it in his memory. He can donate many things and does not pocket even a small profit. Once he becomes a master he has superior capacity, is free from desire, and resides in a solitary place with little lust. His mind always aspires for superior things, and is inclined to annihilationism. His eyes are always malicious. His speech is truthful, and his statements clear. He has few close friends and is steadfast in his acts. He memorizes things firmly and does not forget. His muscle power is strong. His shoulders and chest are beautifully large, his forehead wide, and his hair neat. His mind is firm and hard to subdue. He quickly grasps things and does not forget easily. He can detach himself, but [whenever he commits transgressions] he tends to commit grave transgressions. Such are the marks of a resentful person.

The marks of a stupid person are as follows: He doubts much, regrets much, is lazy, and has no opinion [of his own]. He is satisfied with himself and difficult to convince. He is [also] arrogant and does not accept [good advice]. He does not believe what is to be believed but believes what is not to be believed. He does not know to be [truly] respectful and believes in whatever [he encounters]. He shamelessly and rudely bustles about to many masters. He is thoughtless in his behavior, resists teachings, and is crooked. He does not choose close friends [properly], nor does he ornament himself. He is fond of following non-Buddhist masters and cannot discriminate between the right and the evil.[5] He has difficulty in learning [things] and easily forgets them. He is dull in his capacity and is lazy. He blames those who practice generosity and has no mercy in his mind. He destroys the Dharma-bridge[6] and does not understand what he encounters. With eyes wide open, he sees nothing, and he lacks intelligence. He seeks and desires much. He is doubtful and has little faith. He hates good people and slanders the [law of] retribution for sinful and meritorious [deeds]. He cannot distinguish good words [from bad ones], nor can he understand faults. He does not accept admonitions, and [thus even his] relatives abandon and hate him. He does not know courtesy and likes to speak ill of [other people]. His beard, hair, and nails are long, and his teeth and clothes are dirty. He is exploited by others.

He is not afraid in fearful situations. He is distressed in pleasant situations and is pleased in distressing situations. He laughs in sad situations and is sad in laughable situations. He follows when he is led, and he can endure painful things. He cannot discriminate flavors, nor can he attain detachment easily.

271c He commits serious transgressions. Such are the marks of a stupid person.

If lust is predominant [in a practitioner], he should be cured by the method of impurities. If anger is predominant, he should be cured by the method of friendliness. If stupidity is predominant, he should be cured by the method of meditation on dependent origination (*pratītyasamutpāda*). If discursive thoughts are predominant, he should be cured by the method of mindful breathing. If one is equally [troubled with multiple problems], he should be cured by the method of calling the Buddha to mind. Thus these various diseases are cured by respective [five corresponding] methods.

First: The Method of Curing Lust

A practitioner who has much lust practices the meditation on the impurities. From the feet to the hair, [the whole body] is filled with impurities. (1) Head hair, (2) body hair, (3) nails, (4) teeth, (5) thin skin, (6) thick skin, (7) blood, (8) flesh, (9) tendons, (10) vessels, (11) bones, (12) marrow, (13) liver, (14) lungs, (15) heart, (16) spleen, (17) kidney, (18) stomach, (19) large intestine, (20) small intestine, (21) feces, (22) urine, (23) nasal mucus, (24) saliva, (25) sweat, (26) tears, (27) dirt, (28) dust, (29) pus, (30) brain, (31) placenta, (32) gallbladder, (33) water, (34) thin skin, (35) fat, and (36) meninges. These sorts of impurities are in the body.

Further, the meditation on the impurities consists of [the following nine stages: namely] the visualization of (1) blue pus, (2) swelling, (3) bursting, (4) shedding blood, (5) besmearing [of the blood], (6) stinking pus, (7) being devoured [by scavengers] but not completely consumed, (8) scattering of the bones, and (9) scorched [bones]. [Together,] this is called "the meditation on the impurities."

Further, a lustful person has seven types of attachments; namely attachment to (1) pleasant colors, (2) beautiful appearances, (3) deportment, (4) voices, (5) smoothness of touch, (6) people, or (7) all of these.

(1) If one is attached to pleasant colors, one should practice the meditation on blue pus. [The meditation on] yellowish or reddish impure colors will also [serve for the same purpose]. (2) If one is attached to beautiful appearances, one should practice the meditation on a swelling body and scattering bones. (3) If one is attached to deportment, one should practice the meditation on the bones of a recently dead person smeared with blood. (4) If one is attached to voices, one should practice the meditation on [someone who is] dying with his throat being choked. (5) If one is attached to smoothness of touch, one should practice the visualization of bones and the meditation on the disease of dry skin. (6) If one is attached to people, one should practice [these] six meditations. (7) If one is attached to all of these, one should practice all of these meditations. At times one does various meditations in turn. This is called the meditation on the impurities.

Question: If the body is impure and like a stinking corpse, how does one develop attachment to it? If one is attached to a pure body, one should also be attached to a stinking and rotten body. If one is not attached to a stinking body, one should not be attached to a pure body; for the two (i.e., pure and impure) bodies are equal.

Answer: If one seeks for the two as substantial [elements], neither purity [nor impurity] is perceivable. People's minds are deluded and covered up with perverted views. Thus one considers the impure to be pure. If the perverted mind is destroyed, one attains the meditation on the reality of [all] elements. Then one knows that the impure is unreal and false.

[Further, a corpse has no heat, no life, no consciousness, and no sense faculties. [When] one clearly knows this, one's mind is not attached [to it]. Because the body has heat, life, consciousness, and unimpaired sense faculties, one's mind is delusively attached to it.] Also, when one's mind is attached to [a pleasant] appearance, one considers it to be pure. When the attachment ceases, one knows it to have been impure. If the [body] were indeed pure, it should be always pure. This, however, is not the case. It is like a dog that eats excrement and thinks it is pure, but a human being sees it and thinks it is extremely filthy.

272a

Inside and outside the body, there is nothing pure anywhere. If one is attached to the external [appearance] of the body, [consider that] thin skin covers up the whole body and barely [conceals impurities], like [the skin of] a mango, but that [the body is] still impure. How much more so the thirty-six items inside the body?

[Further, if one considers the causes and conditions for the body, they are all impure. [The body] arises from a combination of impure semen and "blood" of the parents. Once a body is formed, it constantly discharges impurities. Clothing and bedding are also foul-smelling and impure. How much more so a place where someone is dead.

From these reasons, one should know that inside and outside the body, whether alive or dead, everything is impure. *(What follows until the beginning of the second method is the text of a sutra.)*[7]

Also, there are three classes of meditation: introductory, intermediate, and advanced practice.

If [the practitioner] is at the introductory level, [the master] should teach that person as follows: "Create an image of broken skin. Remove impurities and visualize a man of red bones. Fix your mind and meditate, without letting your mind be distracted by other objects. If your mind is distracted, you should concentrate it and return it [to the original objects of meditation]."

If [the practitioner] is at the intermediate level, [the master] should teach him as follows: "Remove the skin and flesh in your imagination. Meditate on the skull exhaustively, without letting your mind be distracted by other objects. If your mind is distracted, you should concentrate it and return it [to the original object of meditation]."

If [the practitioner] is at the advanced level, [the master] should teach him as follows: "[First, mentally] remove the skin and flesh [and reveal] the heart of 'one inch' in the body, and [then] fix your mind to five spots: head, forehead, the area between the brows, the tip of the nose, and the heart. Put your mind on these five spots and meditate on the bones without letting your mind be distracted by other objects. If your mind is distracted, you should concentrate it and return it [to the original objects of meditation]."

One should always mindfully observe the mind, and if the mind is distracted, one should control it. If the mind is exhausted, it will be fixed on the objects of mindfulness. It will abandon other objects and stay [there]. It is just like a monkey that becomes quiet only after it has been tied to a pole for a long time. The object is like a pillar, mindfulness like ropes and chains, and the mind is compared to a monkey. It is also like a nursemaid, who always watches the baby without letting it fall. A practitioner should watch his mind in the same way; he should control the mind step by step and fix it on the object of meditation.

If one's mind is fixed for a long time, it conforms to the state of meditation. If one attains meditation, there are three signs: (1) The body becomes comfortable, soft, and light; (2) white bones emit rays of light like white jade; (3) the mind becomes tranquil. This is called the meditation on the pure. At that time, one obtains the mind [belonging to] the realm of form (*rūpa-dhātu*). These are called the first signs of meditation practice.

If one obtains the mind [belonging to] the realm of form, the mind conforms to the state of meditation, which is an attribute of the realm of form. The mind attains this attribute, but the body rests in the realm of desire (*kāma-dhātu*). The four gross elements become soft and comfortable to the fullest extent. The complexion is pure, shining, and agreeable. Namely, one attains the joy and comfort [belonging to the first stage of meditation].[8]

The second [sign] is that, during the aforementioned meditation on the bones, when one visualizes the image of white bones, rays of light illuminate universally and turn everything into pure white.

The third [sign] is that the mind is fixed on one spot, which is called pure meditation. Since one removes the flesh and observes the bones, [this meditation] is called pure meditation.

These three signs can be perceived by oneself but not by others.

Among the aforementioned three levels of practitioners, an elementary practitioner refers to someone who has not yet made a resolve [to practice Buddhist meditation]; an intermediate practitioner refers to someone who has practiced for three or four lifetimes; an advanced practitioner is someone who has practiced for one hundred years with his own body.

272b

Second: The Method of Curing Anger

If anger is predominant, one should practice three types of cultivation of friendliness: introductory, intermediate, and advanced practice.

If [the practitioner] is at the introductory level, [the master] should teach him as follows: "Extend friendliness to people one likes. How does one extend friendliness to people one likes and wish to give them comfort? If a practitioner obtains various comfortable things for body and mind, such as clothing when it is cold, coolness when it is hot, food and drink when one is hungry and thirsty, richness when one is poor, rest when one has traveled too much, the practitioner wishes [to extend] these comforts to people he likes. One can fix the mind on friendliness, without letting one's mind be distracted by other objects. If the mind is distracted, [one should] concentrate it and return it [to the original object of meditation]."

If [the practitioner] is at the intermediate level, [the master] should teach him as follows: "Extend friendliness to neutral people. How does one extend friendliness to neutral people and give them comfort? If a practitioner obtains various comfortable things for body and mind, the practitioner wishes that neutral people acquire them. One can fix the mind on friendliness and does not let the mind be distracted by other objects. If the mind is distracted, [one should] concentrate it and return it [to the original object of meditation]."

If [the practitioner] is at the advanced level, [the master] should teach him as follows: "Extend friendliness to hostile people. How does one extend friendliness to them and give them comfort? If a practitioner obtains various comfortable things for body and mind, the practitioner wishes that hostile people obtain them. Thus the practitioner can view [hostile people and] people he likes in the same way. [If] one attains the mind equal [to any kind of people], one's mind will be greatly purified. Thus one can widely give comfort to a boundless number of people in the world, whether they are intimate, neutral, or hostile. [If one views everyone] in the ten directions equally, [one's] mind will be greatly purified. One sees sentient beings in the ten directions like seeing oneself. With the mental eye, one vividly sees those sentient beings obtain comfort. At that time one attains the concentration on friendliness."

Question: One might wish that intimate or neutral people obtain comfort. How can one be friendly to hostile people and wish to give them comfort?

Answer: One should give them comfort. Why? [One should think as follows:] "They also have various good points and causes of pure elements. How can I ignore their good [elements] merely because of one [instance of] antagonism?" One should further think as follows: "They might have been my friends in past lives. How can I develop further hatred from [my] present anger? I should be patient with them. This is for my own benefit."

One should also reflect that the benevolent virtue of the practice contains the boundless, vast power of friendliness, and that one should not lose it.

One should also contemplate as follows: "If there were no hostile people, how could I cultivate patience? Giving rise to patience depends on hostile people, and thus hostile people are my benefactors. Also, the retribution for anger is most grave, and thus anger is the worst of all evils; nothing surpasses anger in seriousness. When one extends anger to others, the harm is hard to control. Though one wishes to burn others, in fact one harms oneself."

Further, one reflects this way: "Outside one wears a Dharma robe, and inside one practices patience. Such a person is called a monk. How can he use a harsh voice, show [an angry] face, and cover up his mind? Moreover, the five aggregates are thickets of various suffering and the target of evils. When suffering comes, how can one escape from it? Just like thorns that prick the body, the thorns of suffering are boundless. Hostile people are so many that one cannot rid oneself of them. One should protect oneself and put on leather sandals of patience." As has been said by the Buddha: 272c

If one repays anger with anger, the anger will come back to oneself. If one does not repay anger, one can defeat a great army.

Being free from anger is a characteristic of a great person. The anger of a petty person is immovable like a mountain.

15

Anger is a serious poison that harms many people. If one cannot destroy it, one will harm oneself and perish.

Anger is a great darkness, in which even a person with an eye [for the truth] cannot see. Anger is dust, which taints the pure mind.

Thus one should immediately remove anger; if a poisonous snake is in a room, and if one does not remove it, it will harm people.

Likewise, various poisons of anger are boundless. One should always cultivate friendliness and remove anger.

Thus is the method of the concentration on friendliness.

Third: The Method of Curing Ignorance

If ignorance is predominant, one should practice three stages of contemplation: introductory, intermediate, and advanced practice.

If [the practitioner] is at the introductory level, [the master] should teach him as follows: birth (*jāti*) conditions old age and death (*jarā-maraṇa*); ignorance (*avidyā*) conditions conduct (*saṃskāra*). One [should] contemplate this way without letting one's mind be distracted by other objects. If one's mind is distracted, [one should] concentrate it and return it [to the original objects of meditation].

If [the practitioner] is at the intermediate level, [the master] should teach him as follows: conduct conditions consciousness (*vijñāna*); consciousness conditions "name" and form (*nāma-rūpa*); "name" and form condition the six realms of cognition (*ṣaḍāyatana*); the six realms of cognition condition contact (*sparśa*); contact conditions sensation (*vedanā*); sensation conditions attachment (*tṛṣṇā*); attachment conditions grasping (*upādāna*); grasping conditions existence (*bhava*).[9] One should contemplate this way without letting one's mind be distracted by other objects. If the mind is distracted, [one should] concentrate it and return it [to the original objects of meditation].

If [the practitioner] is at the advanced level, [the master] should teach him as follows: ignorance conditions conduct; conduct conditions consciousness; consciousness conditions "name" and form; "name" and form condition the six realms of cognition; the six realms of cognition condition contact; contact conditions sensation; sensation conditions attachment; attachment conditions grasping; grasping conditions existence; existence conditions birth; birth conditions old age and death. One should contemplate this way without letting one's mind be distracted by other objects. If the mind is distracted, [one should] concentrate it and return it [to the original objects of meditation].

Question: All wise people have wisdom, and all the others lack wisdom. Here, what is meant by "lack of wisdom" (i.e., ignorance)?

Answer: Ignorance means complete lack of understanding. Ignorance can bring about one's existence in the next life. If [wisdom] exists, [future lives] will not exist, but if [wisdom] does not exist, [future lives] will exist. Abandoning the good, grasping the evil, [ignorant people] destroy the reality [of elements] and are attached to delusion. As is said in the "Chapter on the Aspects of Ignorance":[10]

> Not understanding elements that cover up oneself, and not knowing virtuous karma,[11] one makes causes for binding defilements, like a fire that arises from kindling.

> [Due to ignorance] one's mind is attached to bad elements and abandons good elements. [Ignorance] is a thief who steals wisdom from sentient beings; even past and future wisdom is stolen.

> [Due to ignorance] one conceives the five aggregates as permanent, blissful, having self, and pure; nor can one understand the teachings of suffering, origin, extinction, and path (i.e., Four Noble Truths). 273a

> A blind person follows various difficult paths of distress. Because of defilements karma is accumulated, and because of karma suffering evolves.

> Such a person takes things that ought not to be taken and conversely abandons things that ought to be taken. Running in darkness and following a wrong path, such a person will stumble over a stump and fall on the ground.

> A person who has [physical] eyes but no wisdom can be compared to this blind person. When this condition (i.e., ignorance) ceases, the illumination of wisdom appears like the rising sun.

Thus in brief [I have described only the meditation on ignorance]. [All the items] from ignorance up to old age and death should be understood in the same way.

Question: The [theory of] dependent origination in Buddhism is profound. How can an ignorant person observe dependent origination?

Answer: There are two types of ignorant people, one being those who are like cattle or sheep, the other being those who hold onto wrong views. For [the latter type of] ignorant people who are obscured by delusion and hold onto wrong views, the Buddha taught that they should practice concentration by observing dependent origination.

Fourth: The Method of Curing Discursive Thoughts

If discursive thoughts are predominant, one should practice the method of the concentration on [mindful] inhalation and exhalation. (SauN 15.64) There are three levels of practitioners: introductory, intermediate, and advanced.

If [the practitioner] is at the introductory level, [the master] should teach him in the following way: "Concentrate on mindfully counting inhalations and exhalations. Whether the breathing is long or short, count it from one to ten."

If [the practitioner] is at the intermediate level, [the master] should teach him as follows: "Following the breath coming in and out, you should count [your breaths] from one to ten. Your mindfulness and your breathing should be kept together, and your mind should be fixed on one point."

If [the practitioner] is at the advanced level, [the master] should teach him as follows: "Counting the breath, following the breath, fixing the mind on one point, contemplation, shifting, and purification. The concentration on [mindful] inhalation and exhalation have these six methods and sixteen aspects."

"What is the method of counting the breath? [The practitioner is] single-mindedly aware of inhalations. When an inhalation is over, you should count it as 'one.' When an exhalation is over, you should count it as 'two.' If you count the number when the inhalation or exhalation is not over, it is miscounting. If you count from two to nine and then miscount, you have to start over from one. This is just like an accountant who gets two by adding one and one, gets four by adding two and two, and then gets nine by adding three and three."

Question: Why should one count [the breath]?

Answer: [Counting the breath] allows one to realize impermanence easily, allows one to sever discursive thoughts, and allows one to attain single-mindedness. Although body and mind arise and cease and are impermanent, since they continue in similar forms, their impermanence is hard to perceive. [By contrast,] inhalation and exhalation arise and cease [palpably] and their impermanence is easy to realize. Also, by fixing the mind on counting, one can sever discursive thoughts. Discursive thoughts include thoughts of lust, anger, harm, relatives, lands, and immortality.

One who wishes to purify one's mind and enter the correct path should first remove the three types of coarse thoughts, and then the three types of subtle thoughts. After removing the six types of thoughts, one will attain all pure elements. (SauN 15.67) It is just like a gold miner who first removes 273b coarse pebbles, then fine sand, and finally gets refined gold dust. (SauN 15.66)

Question: What are the coarse diseases, and what are the subtle diseases?

Answer: Thoughts of lust, anger, and harm; these three are called coarse diseases. Thoughts of relatives, land, and immortality; these three are called subtle diseases. After removing these thoughts, one attains all pure elements.

Question: One who has not attained awakening has not severed binding defilements. These six types of thoughts are powerful and disturb people at will. How can one sever them?

Answer: If the mind is averted from the world, correct observation can suppress binding defilements, though it cannot uproot them. When one attains undefiled awakening later, one can uproot binding defilements. What is correct observation?

One sees that, for a lustful person, seeking for something is painful; attaining and guarding something is also painful; losing something and regretting it is also greatly painful. Even if the mind obtains the desired object, the mind is not satisfied, which is painful. (SauN 15.9)

Desire is impermanent, vain, and conducive to distress. Everyone has such [desire]; one should realize and abandon it. If a poisonous snake enters one's chamber, and if one does not remove it immediately, one will certainly be harmed. (SauN 15.8)

Unstable, unreal, and valueless is the perverted pleasure of various desires (SauN 15.11). As an arhat with six supernatural powers taught his lustful disciple in the following way: "You should not break the precepts [but maintain] them in purity. Nor should you stay with a woman in the same chamber. Poisonous snakes of binding desires fill the chamber of your mind; entangling attachment will never leave.

"[Even though] you know that the precepts on bodily conduct should not be broken, your mind constantly stays with the fire of lust. You are a practitioner who has left your family and is seeking awakening. How could you indulge your mind so much?

"Your parents gave birth to you, cherished you, and brought you up, and your relatives had both favor and affection for you. All of them cried and tried to dissuade you [from leaving the family]. You could even abandon and disregard [such great affection].

"Nevertheless your mind always entertains lustful thoughts; it wishes to play with them without aversion. It always enjoys being with the fire of lust; [the mind] rejoices in the pleasure of attachment and does not leave it even for a moment."

Thus one should fault lustful thoughts in various ways. These sorts of correct observations remove lustful thoughts.

Question: How does one eliminate thoughts of anger?
Answer:

Since [the time] one was born from within the womb, [life] has always been painful. In this [painful life], people should not develop anger and harmful thoughts.

If you entertain anger and harmful thoughts, friendliness and compassion disappear. Friendliness and compassion on the one hand and anger and harmful thoughts on the other are not comparable. If you cherish friendliness and compassion, anger and harmful thoughts disappear, like brightness and darkness that cannot occupy the same place. (SauN 15.12–13)

If you keep the pure precepts but entertain anger, you destroy the benefit of the Dharma by yourself. It is just like elephants that smear their bodies with mud after bathing in water. (SauN 15.14)

People always have old age, disease, and death, and [experience] hundreds of thousands of sufferings [as if beaten with] various whips and rods. How can a good person, while keeping sentient beings in mind, add [his] anger and harmful thoughts to their suffering? (SauN 15.15)

273c

If you give rise to anger and wish to harm someone, before reaching that person [the anger] will burn yourself. (SauN 15.16)

For these reasons, you should always apply your mind to practicing friendliness and compassion. Do not let anger, harmful thoughts, and evil intentions arise in your mind. (SauN 15.17)

If one always mindfully practices the good elements, one's mind always emulates the thoughts of the Buddha. (SauN 15.18)

For these reasons, one should not pay any regard to evil; [instead] one should always reflect on good elements and gladden one's mind. Then one will attain happiness in this life as well as in the next; one will further attain the eternal happiness of awakening, which is nirvana. (SauN 15.19)

If evil thoughts are accumulated in one's mind, one loses one's own benefits and harms others. (SauN 15.20)

That is why people say that the evil is detrimental to both oneself and others, because it effaces the pure minds of other people. (SauN 15.21)

It is just like a practitioner in the wilderness who raises his hands, cries, and says, "A thief robbed me!"

Someone asks, "Who robs you?"

[The practitioner] replies, "Thieves of possessions I do not fear. I do not collect possessions or seek worldly benefits. What thieves of possessions can rob me? I, however, do collect roots of merit and Dharma jewels. Discursive thoughts, like thieves, come to me and destroy my benefits. Thieves of possessions can be avoided, because there are many storehouses. When, on the other hand, thieves of merit come, there is no way to avoid them."

One should fault anger in these various ways. These sorts of various correct observations remove thoughts of anger.

Question: How does one eliminate thoughts of harming others?

Answer: Hundreds of thousands of types of diseases constantly visit in turn and torment sentient beings. Death, like an enemy, catches people and always tries to kill them. Thus beings are plunged into boundless suffering.

How can a good person cause beings additional harm [by] slandering and plotting to hurt them mercilessly? [If he does such a thing,] the harm will not reach the intended person but return to himself. If a layman gives rise to harmful thoughts, that might be admissible.

This is a worldly practice and becomes a cause for bad karma, but [a layman] does not claim that he cultivates good. If a practitioner who has left his family and is seeking pure awakening gives rise to anger and entertains envious mind,

He lights a violent fire in cool clouds. Know that the evil sin of this act is extremely serious. If a practitioner in the wilderness gives rise to envy, there is an arhat who can read other people's minds.

[The arhat] gives [that practitioner] instructions and bitterly reprimands him, saying: "How foolish you are! Envy naturally destroys your roots of merit. If you seek alms, you should by yourself collect roots of merit and adorn yourself [with them].

"If you do not keep the precepts, nor [practice] meditation or [engage in] much learning, and if you destroy your Dharma body by falsely wearing a dyed robe,[12] you are just an evil beggar. How can you seek alms and benefit yourself?

"Sentient beings are always harmed by hundreds of thousands of sufferings, such as hunger, thirst, cold, and heat. Their bodily and mental agonies are endless. How can a good person do additional harm to them?

"Doing so is just like piercing ailing wounds with a needle. It is also   274a
like a prisoner who is on trial but has not yet been sentenced. His
body is entangled in pain and agonies accumulate [in him]. How can
a friendly and compassionate [person] aggravate his agonies?"

Thus one should fault thoughts of harming others in various ways. These
sorts of various correct observations remove thoughts of harming others.

Question: How does one eliminate thoughts of relatives?

Answer: [The practitioner] should reflect in the following way. Beings
in samsara are drawn by their own karma through the world-systems. Who
are relatives, and who are not? Merely owing to one's ignorance, one erro-
neously develops attachment and believes someone to be one's relative.
(SauN 15.31) Strangers in the past have become relatives, and strangers [in
this life] will become relatives in the future. Relatives in this life were strangers
in the past. (SauN 15.32) It is just like birds that flock together on one tree
in the evening but fly away [from each other] the [next] morning according
to their respective conditions. (SauN 15.33) Families and relatives are the
same way. (SauN 15.34) Born in this world, individual people have separate
minds. They become relatives because conditions meet, and they become
distant because conditions disperse. There are no stable causes, conditions,
fruits, or retribution that keep people together. It is just like a lump of dry
sand grasped in the hand. Conditioned by grasping, it stays together; but conditioned by releasing, it is scattered. (SauN 15.35) Parents bring up children
[thinking that they] will be rewarded in their old age. Children should repay
[their parents later] because they have been embraced and brought up [by
them]. (SauN 15.36) If [relatives] comply with one's mind, they become
close, but if they are against one's mind, they become enemies. (SauN 15.37)
There are relatives who do more harm than good, and there are strangers
who do great service and no harm. People develop affection due to causes
and conditions, and the affection is severed due to causes and conditions.
(SauN 15.38) Just like painters who paint women and are attached to their
own [paintings], one develops one's own attachments and is attached to external objects. (SauN 15.39) What can the relatives in your past lives do for
you in this life? You also cannot benefit your relatives in the past, nor can
they benefit you. Neither [you nor your former relatives] can benefit each

other. (SauN 15.40) In vain one regards others as relatives or strangers. In these world-systems, [in fact the distinction between relatives and strangers] is indefinite, and there is no [clear] boundary [between them]. (SauN 15.41)

As an arhat teaches a novice disciple who has attachment for his relatives, saying: "You are like a foul person who vomits up food and wants to eat it again. You have already left your family. How can you still be attached to it? Your tonsured head and dyed robe are marks of deliverance. Attached to your relatives, you cannot attain deliverance and, on the contrary, are bound by the attachment. The triple world is impermanent, ever changing, and indeterminate. Whether [someone is] a relative or a stranger, [that distinction is only temporary]. Even if some people are relatives now, they will cease to be so in the long run. In this way the sentient beings in the ten directions transmigrate. Relatives are indeterminate, and they are not [eternally] your relatives.

"When a person is about to die, he has no mind or consciousness. He looks straight ahead and does not turn [his eyes]. His breathing stops, and the life expires. It is just like falling into a dark hole. At that time, where are the relatives and family members?

"When a person is newly born, strangers in the past life have been forcibly gathered to become relatives. When he dies, again they cease to be relatives."

Thus contemplating, one should not be attached to relatives.

When a child dies, parents in the three realms cry at the same time. The parents, wife, and children in heaven consider those in the human realm to be false.[13] The parents among *nāga*s consider those in the human realm to be false.

274b

These sorts of various correct observations remove thoughts of relatives.

Question: How does one eliminate thoughts of lands?

Answer: If a practitioner thinks that a land is prosperous, peaceful, and is inhabited by many good people, he is constantly drawn, as by a rope, by thoughts of lands that lead people to the place of transgressors.[14] (SauN 15.42) Realizing that one's own mind is in such a state, if one is a wise person, one should not be attached to [thoughts of lands]. Why? It is because lands are [always] burned by [people's] various faults. (SauN 15.43) Because seasons change, and because there are famines that exhaust [people's] bodies, there is no land whatsoever that is constantly peaceful. (SauN 15.44) In addition, there is no land that is free from the suffering of old age, disease, and death.

(SauN 15.46) Leaving the bodily suffering of this place, one will encounter [other] bodily suffering at another place. Any land one goes to, one will not be freed from suffering. (SauN 15.47) Even if there is a land that is peaceful and prosperous, if there are binding agonies that cause suffering in one's mind, it is not a good land. (SauN 15.48) If a land could remove evil, if it could attenuate binding defilements, and if it could free the mind from agonies, [that land] would be called a good land.[15] All sentient beings have two sorts of suffering: bodily and mental suffering. [Since] constantly there are agonies, [we know that] there is no land where these two sorts of suffering do not exist. (SauN 15.49)

In addition, there are lands that are extremely cold, lands that are extremely hot, lands that are stricken with famine, lands that are plagued with diseases, lands that have many thieves, and lands that are not ruled properly. One should not be attached to these sorts of evils of lands in one's mind. (SauN 15.45)

These sorts of various correct observations remove thoughts of lands.

Question: How does one eliminate thoughts of immortality?

Answer: [The master] should teach the practitioner as follows: If one is born in a good family, if one belongs to an eminent clan, or if one's talents and skills are superior to those of others, one should not pay any regards to them. Why?

When death visits all people, it comes regardless of one's age, status, talents, or power. This body constitutes the causes and conditions of all [forms of] distress and agony. Anyone who feels at peace by thinking that one is young and has a long lifespan is foolish. (SauN 15.54–55) Why? This [body] as the cause for distress and agony is based on the four gross elements. The material elements composed of the four gross elements do not harmonize with each other, like four poisonous snakes. Who can be peaceful? (SauN 15.56) Breathing out, one expects to breathe in, but there is no assurance of this. (SauN 15.57) Further, when one goes to bed, one expects to wake up without fail; this matter is also hard to rely on. (SauN 15.58) From the [moment of] conception until old age, fatal accidents always come to seek moments of death [for beings]. [Even if these accidents] say:[16] "You will never die," who can put faith in this? [Fatal accidents] are like murderers who draw out swords and fit arrows, constantly seeking to kill people without mercy. (SauN 15.59) To the people who are born in this world, nothing is stronger than the power of death. Nothing wins over the strong power of death. Even the most distinguished person of the past could not escape from death. In the present also, there is no wise person who can win over death. (SauN 15.60) Neither gentle entreaty nor cunning deception can help one evade death.

274c   Nor can keeping precepts or diligence turn away death. (SauN 15.61) For these reasons, you should know that [the fate of] human beings is always precarious and cannot be relied upon. Do not [erroneously] believe in permanence and think that your life will last long. Death, as a murderer, always takes people away; it does not wait for old age to kill people. (SauN 15.62)

As an arhat teaches a disciple who is troubled by various thoughts by saying: "Why do you not understand [the significance of] leaving the world and entering religious life? Why do you generate these thoughts? Some people die before birth. Some people die when being born. [There are also people who die] while being nursed, in the weaning period, during childhood, in the prime of life, and in old age. All stages of life are mixed with the realm of death. It is just like a blossom of a tree that sometimes falls when in bloom, sometimes when its fruit has ripened, sometimes when [the fruit] is still immature. Therefore, know that one should make effort and diligently seek for peaceful awakening. Since you are in the company of a powerful murderer, [your life is] unreliable. This murderer skillfully hides himself like a tiger. Thus the murderer of death always seeks to kill people. Everything in the world is empty like a bubble. How could one say that one will wait until the right time and enter religious life? Who could testify that you will definitely [live until you] become old and can practice the path? It is just like a big tree on a cliff, which is being blown by heavy winds above and whose foundation is eroded by big waves below. Who could trust that this tree will remain long? Human life is exactly the same; it is unreliable even for a short period. Father is like a grain; mother like a good field; causes, conditions, transgressions, and merits in the past are like rainfall. Sentient beings are like grains, and samsara is like harvesting.

"Various deities and human kings have wisdom and virtue. For example, Heavenly King [Indra] assists deities, defeats the army of combative demons (*asuras*), and enjoys various pleasures, highest honor, and great light. [Even he] will [eventually] fall back to darkness. Therefore, do not rely on life and say, 'I will do this today. I will do that later.'"

These types of various correct observations remove thoughts of immortality.

Thus one first removes the coarse thoughts and then the subtle thoughts. The mind is purified, and one attains correct awakening. All binding defilements are exhausted, by which one attains a peaceful abode. This is called the fruit of entering religious life. The mind becomes free, and the threefold karma (i.e., bodily, verbal, and mental actions) becomes ultimately pure; thus one will not be reborn again. One will read various sutras and become learned.

At that time, one will attain rewards. When one thus attains rewards, they are not empty. One defeats the army of demon kings and attains a reputation of the greatest bravery. If one is driven by defilements within the world, one is not called strong. If one can defeat the rogues of defilements, and if one puts off the fire of the three poisons, one will attain cool pleasure, be purified, and sleep peacefully in the woods of nirvana. Pure winds of various types of meditation, moral faculties, powers, and the seven elements of awakening arise in the four [directions]. One will reflect on the sentient beings sunk in the sea of the three poisons. If one has such excellent powers of virtues, one is called strong.

Thus if one's mind is distracted in these ways, one should mindfully inhale and exhale, learn the six methods [of meditation], and sever the [six kinds of] thoughts. For this reason, one should mindfully count the breath.

Question: If one can also sever thoughts by the other four types of med- 275a itations such as [the meditation on] the impurities and calling the Buddha to mind, why does one only count the breath?

Answer: It is because [the objects of] the other meditations are slow and hard to lose, but [the object of] counting the breath is quick and easy to turn away. To illustrate, when one releases cattle, since they are hard to lose, keeping them is an easy business. When one releases monkeys, however, since they are easy to lose, keeping them is a difficult task. The matter is the same here. When counting the breath, the mind cannot think of other things even for a moment. Once the mind thinks of other things, it will lose the number. For this reason, when one first [attempts to] sever thoughts, one should count the breath.

When one has already attained the method of counting, one should practice the method of following [the breath] and sever thoughts. When inhalation is completed, one should follow it without counting "one." When exhalation is completed, one should follow it without counting "two." It is just like a creditor who follows a debtor and does not let him go. Think as follows: "This inhaled air goes out again, but it is not the same thing. Exhaled air comes in again, but it is not the same thing." At that time, one will know that inhalation and exhalation are different. For what reason? Exhalation is warm, but inhalation is cool.

Question: [Is it not that] inhalation and exhalation are one [continuous] breath, because the exhaled air enters again? It is just like water that is warm in one's mouth but becomes cool when spit out; a cool thing gets warm again, and a warm thing further gets cool.

Answer: This is not the case. Because the inner mind moves, breath goes out. Once it has gone out, it ceases to exist. [Because] the nostrils draw in the external air, breath comes in. Once it has come in, it ceases to exist. There is no air that is about to move out, nor is there air that is about to move in.

Furthermore, [one should consider the cases of] young people, adults, and old people. In the case of young people, inhalation is longer. In the case of adults, inhalation and exhalation are of the same [length]. In the case of old people, exhalation is longer. Therefore, [inhalation and exhalation] cannot be one breath.

Also, wind arises near the navel and appears to keep going. Breath goes out of the mouth and nose. Once it goes out, it ceases, just like the wind in bellows that ceases when the bellows are opened. If [the air] is drawn in by means of the mouth and nose, wind enters [the body]; this [wind] arises anew based on causes and conditions. It is just like a fan that produces wind when it meets with various conditions.

At that time, one knows that inhalation and exhalation depend on causes and conditions and are delusive and unreal; they are impermanent [and not free from] arising and ceasing. One should contemplate in the following way: exhalation is drawn in by the mouth and nose as causes and conditions. The causes and conditions of inhalation are brought about by the movement of mind. A deluded person, however, does not know this and thinks that it is his own breath.

Breath is none other than wind, which is not different from external wind. Earth, water, fire, and space are also in the same way. Because these five gross elements come together as causes and conditions, consciousness arises. Therefore, even consciousness is not one's own possession. The five aggregates, the twelve realms of cognition, and the eighteen constituent elements are also in the same way. Knowing this, one follows the breath coming in and going out. For this reason, [this method] is called "following [the breath]."

When one has mastered the method of following, one should practice the method of fixing. The fixing method is to fix the mind to the gates of wind (i.e., the nostrils) and be mindful of inhalation and exhalation, after the mind of counting and following is completed.

Question: For what reason does one fix [one's mind]?

Answer: It is because one [needs to] sever various discursive thoughts, because one [should not] let the mind be distracted, because the mind is unfixed and preoccupied when one counts and follows the breath, because when one fixes [the mind] the mind becomes restful and freed from preoccupations, and because the mind rests at one point. Being mindful of inhalation and exhalation is just like a gatekeeper who stays by the gate and who watches the people going in and out. In the same way, the fixed mind knows that when the breath goes out, it goes from the navel to the heart, chest, throat, and then reaches the mouth and nose. [The fixed mind further knows] that when the breath comes in, it comes from the mouth and nose to the throat, chest, heart, and then reaches the navel. That way one fixes the mind to one spot, and this [method] is called "fixing." 275b

Then, while one practices the method of fixing the mind, one should dwell in [the method of] "contemplation." The five aggregates, which arise and cease when one inhales, are different from those, which also arise and cease when one exhales. Thus, when the mind is disturbed, one should remove the disturbance immediately. One should contemplate single-mindedly and make one's contemplation more intense. This is called the "contemplation" method.

One dispenses with abiding at the gates of wind (i.e., the nostrils) and gives up the method of coarse contemplation. When one gives up the method of coarse contemplation, one knows the impermanence of the breath. This is called the "shifting" contemplation. One contemplates the impermanence of the five aggregates and also reflects on the impermanence of inhalation and exhalation. One sees that the initial breath does not come from anywhere and observes that the subsequent breath also leaves no trace. They come into being because [their] causes and conditions meet, and they cease to exist because [their] causes and conditions disperse. This is called the method of "shifting" contemplation, which removes the five obstacles [of meditation] and various defilements.

Though one attained calming and contemplation before, they were compounded with defilements and impure mind. Now in this pure method, the mind only attains purity [without any defilements mixed in]. Furthermore, the previous contemplation was a practice similar to non-Buddhist teachings of mindful inhalation and exhalation. The present one is a practice close to undefiled wisdom, and, though [still] defiled, it is a good path. This is called "purification."

Next, first one observes part of the application of mindfulness to the body; gradually [one observes] all the applications of mindfulness to the body. Then one practices the application of mindfulness to sensation and to the mind. In these [three types of applications of mindfulness, the practice is] impure and far from undefiled wisdom. So, being mindful of inhalation and exhalation, one observes their sixteen aspects. Thus one attains the stages of "heat," "summit," "recognition," "supremacy in the mundane realm," and further "recognition of the elements of suffering" up to the "awareness of extinction [of all defilements]" of an accomplished practitioner who has nothing [more] to learn. This is called "purification."

Among the sixteen methods, (1) the first practice of inhalation [includes] the sixfold practice of inhalation and exhalation (i.e., counting, following, fixing, contemplation, shifting, and purification).

(2) So does the practice of exhalation.

(3) Single-mindedly one is mindful of inhalation and exhalation [and knows] whether they are long or short. For example, a person running in terror, climbing a mountain, carrying a heavy load, or being upset; in such situations, the breath becomes short. When in times of peril one attains a great relief and joy, acquires profit, or is released from jail, in such cases the breath becomes long. All breaths are classified into two categories: long and short. For this reason it is said: "The breath is long," "The breath is short." Thus [observing the length of the breath], one also practices the sixfold practice of inhalation and exhalation.

(4) Being mindful of the breath pervading the body, one is still mindful of the breaths going out and coming in. One thoroughly observes the exhalations and inhalations within one's body. One perceives the breath pervading the body and filling all pores, down to those on the toes, just like water soaking into sand. When the breath goes out, one perceives the breath pervading all pores, from those on the feet to those on the head, also like water soaking into sand. Just like the air that fills bellows, whether it is going out or coming in, the wind blowing in and out through the mouth and nose [fills the body]. One observes the whole body that the wind fills, like holes of a lotus root [filled with water] and a fishing net [soaked in water]. Further, it 275c is not that the mind only observes the breath coming in and going out through the mouth and nose. [The mind] sees the breath coming in and going out through all pores and the nine apertures [of the body]. Thus one knows that the breath pervades the body.

(5) Eliminating various [unfavorable] physical functions,[17] one is again mindful of inhalation and exhalation. When one first practices [mindful] breathing, if one feels laziness, sleepiness, and heaviness in one's body, one should eliminate them all.

(6) The body becomes light, soft, and fitting for meditation; thus the mind experiences joy. Again by being mindful of inhalation and exhalation, one eliminates laziness, sleepiness, and heaviness of mind. The mind becomes light, soft, and fitting for meditation; thus the mind experiences joy.

Having completed the application of mindfulness to breathing, next one practices the application of mindfulness to sensation. [Namely,] having attained the application of mindfulness to the body, now one further attains the application of mindfulness to sensation; thus one truly experiences joy. Further, having understood the reality of the body, one now wishes to know the reality of the mind and mental functions. For this reason, one experiences joy.

(7) By being mindful of inhalation and exhalation, one experiences comfort. By being mindful of inhalation and exhalation, joy increases; it is called comfort.

Alternatively, the first pleasure that arises in the mind is called joy. The subsequent joy that fills the body is called comfort. Also, the comfortable sensations in the first and second stages of meditation are called joy. The comfortable sensations in the third stage of meditation are called comfort.

(8) When one experiences various mental phenomena, one should also be mindful of inhalation and exhalation. Various types of mind arise and cease: polluted mind, unpolluted mind, distracted mind, concentrated mind, righteous mind, and evil mind. Such aspects of mind are called mental phenomena. When the mind experiences joy, one should still be mindful of inhalation and exhalation.

(9) The joy experienced before arose spontaneously and was not aroused intentionally. Because one is mindful of one's own mind, one is gladdened.

Question: For what reason does one arouse joy intentionally?

Answer: It is because one wishes to cure two types of mind: distracted and concentrated. By putting the mind in such a state [of joy], one can be liberated from defilements. For this reason, one applies one's mindfulness to the elements, and the mind arouses joy.

If the mind is not gladdened [spontaneously], one should diligently gladden the mind.

(10) When the mind is concentrated, one should also be mindful of inhalation and exhalation. If the mind is unsettled, one should forcibly settle it. As is stated in a sutra: "When the mind is settled, that is wisdom. When the mind is scattered, that is not wisdom."

(11) When the mind is emancipated, one should also be mindful of inhalation and exhalation. If the mind is not emancipated [spontaneously], one should forcibly emancipate it. It is just like a sheep that has many cockleburs stuck to it, which one [is trying to] pull out of its wool one by one. Releasing the mind from binding defilements is done in the same way.

This is called emancipation by means of the application of mindfulness to the mind.

(12) Observing impermanence, one should also be mindful of inhalation and exhalation. One observes that the elements are impermanent; they arise and cease; they are empty and without self; when they arise, the elements arise in emptiness, and when they cease, they cease in emptiness; in these [elements] there is no male, no female, no person, no agent, and no recipient. This is the observation in conformity with impermanence.

(13) Observing the emergence and dispersal of conditioned elements, one is mindful of inhalation and exhalation. This is called "emergence and dispersal." [When] conditioned elements emerge in the world, they gather

because causes and conditions met in the past, and they disperse because those causes and conditions cease. Such observation is called the observation of emergence and dispersal.

(14) Observing release from binding desires, one is mindful of inhalation and exhalation. [When] the mind is released from its binding defilements, it will be the supreme element. This is the observation in conformity with the release from desires.

276a

(15) Observing extinction, one is mindful of inhalation and exhalation. The suffering of binding defilements is exhausted wherever one is situated, and the spot [of one's present residence] becomes peaceful. This is the observation in conformity with extinction.

(16) Observing abandonment, one is also mindful of inhalation and exhalation. Abandonment of lust, defilements, the five aggregates consisting of physical and mental [elements], and the conditioned elements: this is the supreme serenity. Such observation is in conformity with the application of mindfulness to the elements.

These are called the sixteen methods.

Fifth: The Method of Curing People Equally [Troubled with Multiple Problems]

The fifth method is a practice [designed] to cure people equally [troubled with multiple problems].[18] [This method is also intended for] people who have committed grave transgressions and who seek for [help from] the Buddha.

[The master] should teach such people the single-minded concentration on calling the Buddha to mind. There are three types of people who practice the concentration on calling the Buddha to mind: elementary, intermediate, and advanced.

If the practitioner is at the elementary level, [the master] should lead him to a statue of the Buddha or teach him to go there by himself and [make him] clearly observe the major and minor bodily marks of the statue. When each mark has become clear [in his mind], he should single-mindedly retain [that mental image] and return to a silent place. [There] he observes the statue of the Buddha with his mental eye and does not let the mind turn away. He fixes his mind on the statue without letting the mind be distracted by other objects.

33

If the mind is distracted, he should concentrate it, so that it is always fixed on the statue. If the mind is not fixed, the master should teach him by saying:

"You should blame your mind [in the following way]: 'The transgressions I have made because of you (i.e., mind) are uncountable. Among the various sufferings in the boundless [realms of] samsara, there is none that I have not experienced. In the hells, I swallowed melted copper and [repeatedly] ate burning iron balls. In the realm of animals, I ate excrement and devoured grass. In the realm of hungry ghosts, I suffered from hunger. In the realm of human beings, I suffered from poverty. In the realm of deities, I was distressed by the [unavoidable] loss of desirable objects. Because I have always followed you, you have made me suffer from these various physical and mental agonies, which were indeed boundless. Now I have to control you. You have to follow me. Now I will fix you on one spot. I shall never again be troubled by you and experience suffering [as before]. You have always troubled me. Now I have to trouble you with this undertaking.'"

If he keeps [practicing] this way without letting his mind be distracted, then he will attain the mental eye and see the rays of light [emanating] from the [major and minor bodily] marks of the Buddhist statue. [The mental image] will be no different from the [image] one sees with one's physical eyes. Thus fixing the mind is called the meditation of an elementary practitioner.

At that time, he should further reflect as follows: "Whose image is this? This is an image of Śākyamuni Buddha in the past. Though I see the statue of the Buddha now, in fact the statue has not come here, nor have I gone there. By mental imagination I saw the past Buddha. When his spirit descended [from Tuṣita Heaven], heaven and the earth quaked. He had the thirty-two major marks of a great person, [namely]:

1. Flat soles
2. Wheels with a thousand spokes on the soles
3. Beautifully long toes
4. Wide heels
5. Webs between the toes and fingers
6. Beautifully high and flat insteps
7. Calves like those of an antelope
8. Hands reaching below the knees while standing upright
9. Hidden male organ

276b

10. Body like a banyan tree
11. Each hair growing from each pore
12. Hair growing upwards and curling clockwise
13. Body color superior to that of fine gold
14. Rays from the body reaching three yards
15. Beautifully thin skin
16. Protuberances on the seven spots [of the body][19]
17. Beautifully flat armpits
18. Upper body like that of a lion
19. Beautifully large and upright body
20. Round shoulders
21. Forty teeth
22. White and even teeth, without gaps and deeply rooted
23. Four big white cuspids
24. Square jaw like that of a lion
25. [Tongue with which to] enjoy the supreme flavors
26. Large, wide, long, and thin tongue
27. Profound voice like that of Brahmā
28. Voice like that of an Indian cuckoo
29. Dark-blue eyes
30. Eyelashes like that of an ox king
31. Topknot made of flesh with bones
32. White and beautifully long tuft of hair, curling clockwise, between the brows."

"Next, the eighty minor bodily marks:
1. Invisible crown [of the head]
2. Beautifully high and straight nose, with invisible nostrils[20]
3. Brows in the shape of a new moon and with the color of dark-blue beryl
4. Beautiful ears
5. Body [as strong as that of] Nārāyana
6. Joints of bones hooked together
7. Body that turns all at once like that of an elephant king
8. Feet that remain four inches above the ground, but that leave footprints when walking

9. Thin and glossy nails of the color of red copper

10. Beautifully round knees

11. Clean body

12. Soft body

13. Straight body

14. Long, round, and delicate fingers

15. Fingerprints like pictures adorned with various colors

16. Deep and invisible veins

17. Deep anklebones invisible [from the outside]

18. Moist and glossy body

19. Upright posture

20. Complete body *(He was conceived in the third month and was born in the second month of the year.)*

21. Proper decorum

22. Peaceful residing place *(He is immovable like a standing ox king.)*

23. Dignity that sways everyone

24. Everyone wishes to see him

25. Wide face

26. Proper complexion with decent color

27. Lips in the color of a *bimba* fruit

28. Well-rounded face

29. Deep and echoing voice

30. Round and deep navel that does not jut out

31. [Body] hairs curling clockwise all over [the body]

32. Complete hands and feet

33. Hands and feet that work at will *(In former translations, it was said: "[The hands can] grasp inward and outward.")*

34. Clear and straight lines on the hands and feet

35. Long lines on the hands

36. Unbroken lines on the hands

37. [Appearance that makes] all sentient beings with wicked minds attain
276c   a joyful countenance upon seeing him

38. Wide and beautiful face

39. Moonlike face

40. [Appearance that does] not terrify or frighten any sentient beings who see him

41. Pores that emit fragrant wind

42. Mouth that emits fragrance and makes sentient beings who smell[21] this enjoy the Dharma for seven days

43. Behavior like that of a lion

44. Deportment like that of an elephant king

45. Gait like a goose king

46. Head like a *madana* fruit *(This fruit is not round or long.)*

47. Voice endowed with all the pitches *(There are altogether sixty pitches of voice, of which the Buddha had them all.)*

48. Sharp cuspids[22]

49. *(There is no Chinese equivalent, so this item is untranslatable.)*[23]

50. Large and red tongue

51. Thin tongue

52. Pure red hair of clean color

53. Wide and long eyes

54. Filled apertures *(The nine apertures [on the body] are all filled up.)*[24]

55. Hands and feet that are red and white like the colors of lotus flowers

56. Belly that is not conspicuous or thrust out

57. Non-protruding belly

58. Immovable body

59. Heavy body

60. Large body

61. Tall body

62. Entirely clean hands and feet

63. Great rays of light from the four sides [of his body] that illuminate [the road] when he walks

64. Equal attitude to [all] sentient beings

65. Not attached to teaching [people], or not craving disciples

66. Volume of the voice adjusted to the size of the audience, neither too big nor too small

67. Preaching according to the language of the audience

68. Unimpeded in speech

69. Sequential preaching

70. Bodily marks that cannot be seen clearly or completely understood by any sentient being

71. [Appearance that does not make] people weary of seeing him
72. Beautifully long hair
73. Beautiful hair
74. Undisturbed hair
75. Unsplit hair
76. Soft hair
77. Hair in the color of blue beryl
78. Done-up hair
79. Not sparse hair
80. *Śrīvatsa* mark on the chest, and *svastika* marks on the hands and feet."

The rays of light [from his body] thoroughly illuminated the boundless worlds. When he was just born, he walked seven steps and uttered essential words. He became a recluse, practiced asceticism, and subdued the armies of demons under the *bodhi* tree. In the twilight of the third watch, he attained correct awakening. The rays of light were clear and illuminated afar, filling the ten directions and reaching everywhere. Deities offered songs [to the accompaniment of] strings in the sky; they further scattered petals and rained perfume. All sentient beings respected him boundlessly. He walked independently by himself in the triple world. When he looked back, he turned his body like an elephant king. He looked at the *bodhi* tree. When he first turned the Dharma wheel, deities attained awakening. He [thus] attained awakening by himself and reached nirvana.

277a   Thus the body of the Buddha impresses [people] boundlessly. One should call the Buddha to mind without being distracted. If one's mind is distracted, [one should] concentrate it and return it [to the original objects of meditation]. Thus one's mind is not disturbed. At that time, one can see one buddha, two buddhas, up to the physical bodies of the buddhas in the boundless worlds in the ten directions. One can see all these with one's mental imagination. Having succeeded in seeing the buddhas, one listens to the words of their preaching. Otherwise, one raises questions by oneself, for whom the Buddha preaches and solves various doubts. If one has mastered [the practice of] calling the Buddha['s body] to mind, one should further call to mind the meritorious Dharma body, boundlessly great wisdom, bottomlessly deep intellect, and immeasurable virtues.

(1) Tathāgata. *(Tathā in Chinese means "thus." The word āgata means "understood" and "true speech." It also means that other awakened sages have come through a peaceful way, and that the Buddha [also] has thus come. Further it means that he does not come to a subsequent existence* [i.e., rebirth in samsara].*)*

(2) Arihan [sic]. *(Ari in Chinese means "enemy." Han means "to kill." Wearing the armor of patience and having the shield of diligence, the Buddha kills arrogance and other enemies with the bow of meditation and the arrow of wisdom. For this reason, he is called "killing enemies.")*

(3) Samyaksambuddha. *(Samyak in Chinese means "true." Sambuddha means "realizing everything." He realizes the suffering, [its] cause, nirvana, and the path leading [to nirvana]. [Thus he] correctly understands that the Four [Noble] Truths cannot be altered. Since he understands [things] exhaustively without leaving anything, he is called someone who has "true realization of everything.")*

(4) Vidyācaraṇa. *(Vidyā in Chinese means illumination. Caraṇa means good practice. Illumination refers to the threefold illuminations. Practice refers to the pure practice. By means of these he has achieved the great awakening by himself, without a master. Therefore he is called [someone who has] illumination and good practice.)*

Sampanna. *(This in Chinese means "fulfillment.")*

(5) Sugata. *(This in Chinese means "having good understanding." It also means "having good and unguided apprehension" or "eloquent without being troubled.")*

(6) Lokavid. *(Loka in Chinese [means "world." Vid] means "wisdom." The wise man [i.e., Buddha] knows the cause of the world and the path to [its] extinction. Therefore this item is called "world-wisdom." "World-wisdom" means "knowing the world.")*

(7) Anuttara. *(This in Chinese means "unsurpassed." [The Buddha has] good character and supramundane wisdom, and he guides all [sentient beings]. [His] great virtues are boundless. Among Brahmās, demons, and accomplished people, there is none who is equal to him. How much less so could there be anyone who surpasses the Buddha. Because [his] virtues are great, one says "unsurpassed.")*

(8) Puruṣadamya. *(Puruṣa in Chinese means "a great person." Damya means "to be [guided]." This refers to the master who guides the people to be guided. The Buddha, because of his great friendliness, compassion, and wisdom, keeps [people] from losing the path under his guidance; sometimes with sweet words, sometimes with harsh words, and sometimes with personal instruction. For this reason, the Buddha is called the master who guides the people to be guided.)*

(9) Śāstā devamanuṣyāṇām. *(This in Chinese means "master of deities and human beings." [The Buddha] can exhaustively release all people from defilements and makes [people] always stay in and not retrogress from the superior elements.)*

(10) Buddha Bhagavān. *(Because the knowledge of the past, present, and future, which had or had not been acquired [previously], were all acquired [under the bodhi tree]. All the elements that had or had not been exhausted [before] were clearly known under the bodhi tree. Therefore, he is called Buddha Bhagavān; namely he has great reputation. Further, bhaga [also] means "female organ." Vam- means "to spit out." Because he has eternally abandoned the female organ, he has "spat out the female organ.")*[25]

Then [the practitioner] further calls to mind in the same way the divine virtues of two buddhas, three, four, five, up to boundless buddhas filling the [whole of] space. Then again [the practitioner] sees only one buddha. [The practitioner] can see that one buddha becomes the buddhas in the ten directions, and that the buddhas in the ten directions become one buddha. He can transform one color into the colors of gold, silver, crystal, and beryl; according to the wish of the people, he can show anything.

At that time, he meditates on only two things: the [Dharma] body of the Buddha [like] space, and the virtues of the buddhas. He has no other thought. The mind attains full control and is not distracted [any more]. This is when the concentration on calling the Buddha to mind is achieved.

If the mind is distracted, and thoughts are on the five sense objects, or if one is occupied with six kinds of thoughts, one should forcibly control the mind and subdue it.

Think thus: existence as a human being is hard to obtain, and the Buddha-Dharma is hard to encounter. Therefore, it is said that the sun is the best among various [kinds of] light, and the Buddha is the best among various wise [people]. For what reason? Because the Buddha gives rise to great compassion always for all people, he [offers even his own] head, eyes, marrow, and brain to save sentient beings. How could one mindlessly neglect [the practice of] calling the Buddha to mind and betray his great favor?

If the Buddha did not emerge in the world, there would be no paths leading to [rebirth as] a human being or deity or to nirvana. If one offers incense and flowers [to the Buddha], or if one erects a stupa [for the Buddha] using one's own bones, flesh, blood, and marrow, one is not equal to a practitioner who makes offerings of the Dharma and attains nirvana. Even [in the last case], one betrays the favor of the Buddha.

[So] even if one's practice of calling the Buddha to mind is entirely fruitless, still one should exert the mind and keep [the Buddha's virtues] in mind without forgetting [them]. Thereby one repays the favor of the Buddha. Needless to say, if one calls the Buddha to mind and thereby acquires various types of concentration and wisdom, and [goes on to] attain buddhahood, and still does not keep [the virtues of the Buddha] in mind devotedly[, it would be a great betrayal of his favor]. Therefore, a practitioner should always devote his mind [to this practice] without letting his mind be distracted. If he can see the Buddha, he can ask him about his doubts. Therefore, [as stated previously,²⁶] calling the Buddha to mind solves [the problem of those who are] equally [troubled with multiple problems] and have [made] other grave transgressions.

Fascicle Two

At that time, though the practitioner has attained "single-mindedness," his power of concentration has not been established. So he is still troubled with the defilements belonging to the realm of desire. He should employ [skillful] means to proceed to the first stage of meditation and eliminate desires.

How can one eliminate [desires]? One should observe the faults of the realm of desire: desire is impure, and [the realm is filled with] various evils. One should call to mind that the first stage of meditation is peaceful and enjoyable. How should one observe desire? Know that desires are impermanent and are enemies of merit. [Desires] are like illusions or magical emanations; they are empty and cannot be grasped. If one thinks of something and has not obtained it, the ignorant mind is already disturbed. How much more so if one has obtained it; the mind will be fettered by and covered up with lustful desire. Even the enjoyable places in the heavens are not always peaceful. How much less so in [the realm of] human beings? The human mind is attached to desire and is never satisfied. It is like a fire that devours wood, or like an ocean that swallows up streams. It is [also] like King Mūrdhagata,[27] who rained the seven types of jewels, ruled over the four continents, and shared a throne with Indra, but still was not satisfied. It is [also] like Nahuṣa *(This is a surname)*, who was a king turning a golden wheel[28] but was pressed by desire and fell into [rebirth as] a serpent. Consider also that even sages who eat fruit, wear grass, and seek awakening secluded deep in the mountains and with their hair unbound cannot be freed from the destructions of the rogues of desire.

The pleasures of desire are very few, and the pains of hatred are numerous. Those who are attached to desire are approached by bad friends and avoided by good friends. Desire is poisonous wine that intoxicates and kills foolish people. Desire is deceit that drives foolish people, who become exhausted and suffer in every corner of their lives, never attaining freedom. Only when they leave their desires, will their bodies and minds be peaceful and their pleasure limitless.

Desire is fruitless, like a dog chewing meatless bones. When one seeks after some desire, one tries hard. Only after taking great pains does one obtain

277c

43

it. Getting it is so hard, but losing it is so easy. It is like relying on a temporary power that cannot last for long. It is [also] like scenes in a dream, which are obscure, and which instantly vanish. Desired objects cause trouble. Seeking them is already painful, and getting them is also painful. The more one gains, the more one suffers. It is like a fire to which new wood are added. The more wood there is, the more intense the fire will be. Desired objects are like a lump of meat for which many birds compete. In short, [desire] is like a moth that flies into fire or like a fish that swallows a hook. It is also like deer that follow the voice[29] or a thirsty person who drinks salty water. All sentient beings get into trouble due to desire; they are not exempt from any type of suffering.

Therefore, one should know that desire is harmful. One should seek the first stage of meditation and put out the fire of desire. The practitioner should single-mindedly, diligently, and faithfully make his mind progress without being distracted. He observes the desirous mind and fully removes the binding defilements. Then he attains the first stage of meditation. He is liberated from the fierce fire of desire and attains the heatless meditation. It is as if one attained shade in the heat, or as if a poor person became rich. At that time, [the practitioner] attains the joyful sentiment of the first stage of meditation. He meditates on various merits in his meditation and observes the mental discrimination of likes and dislikes; thus he attains single-mindedness.

Question: How can we know that a practitioner of meditation has attained single-mindedness?

Answer: His complexion becomes sleek. He walks slowly, quietly, and upright. He does not lose single-mindedness, and his eyes are not attached to appearances. [With] noble virtues and the power of concentration, he does not crave for reputation or profit. He destroys arrogance. His nature is mild and he does not cherish harmful [thoughts]; nor does he have stinginess or envy. He is faithful, and his mind is pure; [thus] he does not dispute with others. He is not deceptive and is easy to talk with. He is gentle, has a sense of shame, and his mind is always directed to the Dharma. He practices diligently and completely upholds the precepts. He chants sutras, correctly remembers them, and practices according to the teachings. His mind is always joyful and does not take offense in offensive situations. Among the four types of donations,[30] he does not accept impure ones. He accepts pure donations, but he knows the [proper] amount and is content with [what he has received]. He wakes up easily and can practice the two types of donations (i.e., material and spiritual). He is patient and removes wickedness. When he debates, he does not get self-contented and speaks little. He is modest and [equally] respects senior, middle, and junior [monks]. He always approaches and follows good masters and friends. He is moderate in eating and drinking and is not attached to the flavors. He likes solitary and quiet places. His mind bears suffering or pleasure without being stirred. He harbors no grudges, [seeks] no competition, and does not like fights. These types of characteristics are those of [someone who has attained] single-mindedness.

These[31] two [mental] elements [in the first stage of meditation], reflection and investigation, disturb the concentrated mind. It is just like pure and quiet water is muddied when waves arise. Thus the practitioner is already concentrated inside but is troubled by reflection and investigation. [However,] like an exhausted person who attains rest or like a sleepy person who gets ease, he then is gradually freed from reflection and investigation and gives rise to pure concentration. He is pure inside and, with joy and comfort, can enter the second stage of meditation. The mind becomes tranquil and silent. He has now attained this joy that he had not attained before.

Then his mind observes that the joy is troublesome, like the aforementioned reflection and investigation. He practices the method of no joy. Thus he attains the comfort of the stage without joy taught by awakened sages. Single-mindedly he is clearly aware, mindful, and equanimous, and thus he can enter the third stage of meditation. Since joy has already been abandoned, [the third stage of meditation has] clear awareness, mindfulness, comfort, and equanimity.[32] Awakened sages talk about comfort and equanimity. Other people have difficulty in abandoning the utmost comfort; [for] there is no greater comfort than this. Therefore, all awakened sages say that in all the pure stages, friendliness is the utmost comfort.

[Even] comfort is troublesome. Why? In the supreme meditation the mind does not operate, because there is no [mental] activity [in it]. If there is any operation, there is change. If there is change, there is suffering. For this reason, [in] the third stage of meditation, comfort is considered to be troublesome.

Further, by skillful means, [the practitioner] abandons such suffering and comfort. He previously got rid of distress and joy, [and now] he removes

278a

45

suffering and comfort. Being equanimous, mindful, and pure, he can enter the fourth stage of meditation, [which does not have] either suffering or comfort [but has] equanimity, pure mindfulness, and single-mindedness. Therefore the Buddha says: "[The stage at which] the most pure equanimity [is attained] is called the fourth stage of meditation." In the third stage of meditation comfort operates, and therefore [the third stage of meditation] is considered [not free from] suffering. For this reason, the fourth stage of meditation, which has removed suffering and comfort, is called the immovable abode.

[The practitioner then] gradually observes the realm of space and destroys the [meditative] images of internal and external matter. He eliminates the images of tangible [objects] and does not create images of various material elements. He observes the realm of boundless space. He always observes the faults of matter and reflects on the superior merits of the absorption belonging to the realm of space. He practices the reflection in this method and attains the realm of [boundless] space.

He [then] reflects on the realm of boundless consciousness and observes the faults of the realm of space. He reflects on the merits of the realm of boundless consciousness. He practices the reflection in this method and attains the realm of [boundless] consciousness.

He [then] reflects on the realm of nothingness and observes the faults of the realm of consciousness. He reflects on the merits of the realm of nothingness. He practices the reflection in this method and attains the realm of nothingness.

He [then] reflects on the realm that is neither with nor without ideation. If [we talk about] all [types of] ideation, problems are manifold; they are like diseases and wounds. If [we talk about the realm] without ideation, it is a realm of ignorance. Therefore, [the realm] neither with nor without ideation is the most peaceful good realm. He observes the faults of the realm of nothingness and reflects on the merits of the realm that is neither with nor without ideation. He practices the reflection in this method and attains the realm that is neither with nor without ideation.

Alternatively, there is a practitioner who starts from the first stage and reaches the advanced stage, and who practices the mind of friendliness even at the advanced stage. First he himself obtains comfort and destroys the poison of anger. Then he extends [the comfort] to boundless sentient beings in the ten directions. Then he attains the concentration on friendly mind.

A compassionate mind takes pity on the suffering of sentient beings and can destroy manifold agonies. He extends [his compassion] widely to boundless sentient beings. Then he attains the concentration on compassionate mind.

278b

[The practitioner] can destroy displeasure and make boundless sentient beings attain joy. Then he attains the concentration on joy.

[The practitioner] can destroy suffering and comfort and observes clearly boundless sentient beings in the ten directions. Then he can attain the concentration on equanimous mind.

In the second stage of meditation, matters are the same. In the third and fourth stages of meditation, joy is excluded.

Then [the practitioner] learns the five supernatural powers, and his body can fly and transform itself at will. The practitioner is single-mindedly absorbed in eagerness, diligence, single-mindedness, and wisdom. Single-mindedly he observes [his] body and always creates the image of lightness and wishes to accomplish flight. Whether big or small *(If the absorption in eagerness surpasses [the ordinary], it is called "big." If the absorption in eagerness is less [than the ordinary], it is called "small")*, it is troublesome. With exceeding diligence, he can always contemplate lightness single-mindedly. It is just like a person who can float [on water] and who does not sink because of his strong willpower, and like a monkey that falls down from a high place but is not hurt because of its strong willpower. In the same way, the power of eagerness, diligence, single-mindedness, and wisdom makes the [body] great. Then the body becomes smaller, and [eventually the practitioner] can carry [his] body.

Next, [the practitioner] observes the element of space in [his] body.[33] He always practices this observation, and the power of eagerness, diligence, single-mindedness, and wisdom becomes extremely large, and thus he can lift up [his] body. It is just like the power of a great wind that blows a heavy thing away to a distant place. The matter is the same here. First he should by himself try to get off the ground for one foot or two feet, and gradually up to ten feet. Then he comes back to the original place. It is like a young bird learning to fly or like a child learning to walk. He reflects and clearly knows that he can go far if his mind-power is strong. He learns to observe the four elements; he removes the earth element and only observes [the other] three elements. If his mindfulness is not carried away, he attains supernatural powers. His body is unhindered and he can fly like a bird. Further, he should learn to imagine that a distant place is nearby, and therefore [something] disappears nearby and appears at a distant place.[34]

Also, he can transform various things. For example, if he observes the earth element in a piece of wood and removes the other elements, the wood becomes earth. For what reason? It is because there is a share of the earth element in the wood. Likewise, [wood can be transformed into] water, fire, wind, space, gold, silver, and jewels. Why? It is because wood has these elements.[35]

This is the foundation of the first supernatural power. The four stages of meditation have fourteen minds of transformation altogether. The first stage of meditation has two fruits (i.e., two possible outcomes): (1) the first stage of meditation, and (2) the realm of desire. The second stage of meditation has three fruits: (1) the second stage of meditation, (2) the first stage of meditation, and (3) the realm of desire. The third stage of meditation has four fruits: (1) the third stage of meditation, (2) the second stage of meditation, (3) the first stage of meditation, and (4) the realm of desire. The fourth stage of meditation has five fruits: (1) the fourth stage of meditation, (2) the third stage of meditation, (3) the second stage of meditation, (4) the first stage of meditation, and (5) the realm of desire.[36] The other supernatural powers are as stated in the Mahayana treatise.[37]

There are two types of people among the disciples of the Blessed One who learn the five methods [of meditation][38] and aspire to attain nirvana: those who prefer concentration because it is comfortable, and those who prefer wisdom because they are afraid of suffering. Those for whom concentration is predominant first learn meditation and then learn nirvana. Those for whom wisdom is predominant head for nirvana directly. Directly heading for nirvana means that, before severing defilements or attaining meditation, one directly seeks nirvana with a devoted and undistracted mind, and transcends lust and other defilements. This is called nirvana.

278c

The body is in fact impermanent, painful, impure, and without self. Due to perverted views on the body, one thinks that it is permanent, blissful, having self, and pure. For this reason, one is attached to one's body on every occasion. This is the lowliest sentient being.

Since the practitioner wishes to destroy his perverted [views], he should practice the observations of the four applications of mindfulness. He observes that the body is impermanent because many sufferings arise [there] depending on their causes and conditions. It is painful because of various agonies. It is impure because the body has thirty-six [filthy] things. It is without self because [the body] does not have autonomous control [over itself]. [The practitioner] practices these types of observations. He observes inside the body, outside the body, and both inside and outside the body. He practices these types of observations. This is called the application of mindfulness to the body. Thus is the reality of the body. For what reason should one give rise to perverted views regarding the [body] and be attached to the body?

One [should] closely contemplate and be mindful of the comfortable sensations of the body. Because one loves its comfortable sensations, one is attached to the body. One should [therefore] observe that these comfortable sensations are in fact not perceivable. Why? Owing to clothing and food, comfort is generated. Excessive comfort, however, gives rise to pain, because [what appears to be comfort] is not truly comfort. When the pain of a wound is stopped by applying medicine, it is called comfort. In comparison to a great pain a small pain is considered to be comfort, but it is not true comfort. Also, because an old pain is considered to be painful, a new pain is considered to be comfort. When one carries a heavy load and moves it from one shoulder to the other, the new weight is considered to be comfort, but it is not true, lasting comfort. In the case of the nature of fire, it is always hot and does not cool down even for a while. If these [examples] were truly comfort, they should not turn into discomfort.[39]

Someone might say that external things are the cause of pleasure, but the [internal] condition (i.e., the state of mind) is not always [conducive to] pleasure. Sometimes it becomes the cause of pleasure, but sometimes it becomes the cause of pain. If one lets one's mind be associated with lust, then [external things are felt to be] pleasant; if with anger, then [these are felt to be] painful, and if with ignorance, then [these are felt to be] neither pleasant nor painful. Inferring from this, we can tell whether there is pleasure or not. [There must be pleasure.]

We respond to this view. There is no [pleasure at all]. Lust cannot be [the condition for] pleasure. Why? If lust (i.e., the alleged condition for pleasure) exists in [ourselves], we would not seek for women outside [ourselves]. [But actually we do] seek for women, therefore we should know that lust is [not the condition for pleasure; it is only] painful. If lust were [indeed the condition for] pleasure, we would not abandon it any time, and if we do abandon it, it cannot be a real [condition for] pleasure.

[Another point is that] we [merely] regard a small pain in [the face of a] larger pain as pleasure. For example, when one is facing execution but [manages to] keep his life and is [merely] whipped, one would regard this as pleasure.

When a lustful mind is vehement, one regards lust as pleasant. But when one gets old and becomes tired of lust, one understands that lust is not pleasant. If [lust] had truly pleasant characteristics, one should not become tired of it. For these various reasons, we cannot truly recognize any pleasant characteristics of lust. When pleasure is lost, it is painful. The Buddha says: "One should observe a pleasant sensation as painful, and a painful sensation as pleasant, as if one were shot with an arrow. One should [observe] a neutral sensation as something impermanent that arises and ceases." Thus far is [the explanation of] the application of mindfulness to sensations.

One should know that mental sensations consist of painful, pleasant, and
279a neutral sensations. What is mind? The mind is impermanent because it arises from causes and conditions, and because, arising and ceasing, it does not abide; [merely] similar [but discrete moments of mind are] arising [in succession]. Only due to perverted [views] does one think that the [mind] is a single [entity]. What did not exist before now exists, and having existed, it will not exist anymore. Therefore, [the mind] is impermanent. One observes the mind as empty. Why? From causes and conditions the eye and a visible object arise. Eye consciousness arises when [the eye and its object] are combined with mindfulness, the wish to see, and other [conditions]. It is just like a lens. When the sun and a lens exist, together with various conditions such as dry grass and cow dung, fire arises. When one examines each [of the relevant elements], fire is not perceivable. [It is just that] when [these] conditions meet, fire arises. Examining [these conditions] one by one, no fire is perceivable. Eye consciousness is also the same. It abides neither in the eye, nor in visible objects, nor somewhere between them. It has no abode, nor is it nonexistent. Therefore the Buddha says: "[Everything] is like an illusion or emanation." If [one] observes the present

mind and the past mind, they are either painful, pleasant, or neutral. Manifold minds cease in their respective ways. One should observe the internal mind, the external mind, and both the internal and external minds[40] in a similar way. Thus far is [the explanation of] the application of mindfulness to mind.

Next, observe to whom this mind belongs. Observe and contemplate the elements associated with mind, such as mindfulness and wishes, and the elements not associated with mind. Clearly observe their proprietor;[41] the proprietor is not perceivable. For what reason? Because [the elements] arise from causes and conditions, [the elements] are impermanent. Because they are impermanent, they are painful. Because they are painful, they have no autonomous control. Because they have no autonomous control, they have no proprietor. Because they have no proprietor, they are empty.

Before, one has observed individually that body, sensations, mind, and elements are all not perceivable. Now one should make the overall observation that, among the [objects] of the four applications of mindfulness, the proprietor is not perceivable. Apart from them, [the proprietor] is not perceivable either.

If [the elements are] permanent, no [proprietor] is perceivable. If [they are] impermanent, no [proprietor] is observable either. If permanent, [things] should be constantly painful or pleasant, and we should not forget things. If the spirit permanently exists, there should be no transgression of killing, and no nirvana. If the body is the spirit, when the impermanent body perishes, the spirit should also perish. [In that case,] there should be no future life, nor should there be transgressions or merits. When one universally observes thus, there is no proprietor. All elements are empty and do not have autonomous control [over themselves]. Because causes and conditions meet, [elements] arise, but when causes and conditions are lost, [elements] cease. Thus elements [depend on] the meeting of conditions. Thus far is [the explanation of] the application of mindfulness to elements.

If the practitioner attains the application of mindfulness to elements, he gets averted from the empty elements of old age, sickness, and death in this world that have nothing permanent, blissful, substantial, and pure. "What shall I seek for among these empty elements? I should rather enter and reside in nirvana that is the supreme element." Since by establishing the power of diligence one attains profound *śamatha (Profound* śamatha *means fixing the mind on one point. There is no corresponding word in this country)*, at that time he attains profound *śamatha*. Residing in the fourth application of mindfulness to elements, he observes that the characteristics of elements are all painful and not pleasant. "No pleasure" is the truth; any other statement is false. The causes of suffering are mental defilements, such as lust, and karma. [Suffering] does not arise from such false notions as "deity," "time," and "sense objects."

279b   These defilements and karma give rise to [multifarious] suffering, and the suffering is entirely exhausted when one enters nirvana. Such false notions as the material and immaterial worlds and the beginning of the world[42] *(Non-Buddhists say that, at the beginning of all elements of existence, matter was the origin of the world. Non-Buddhists say that, for this reason, nirvana also has an origin. That which creates all things is called the creator.)* cannot remove these sufferings. The eightfold straight [path] such as the correct view is the path to nirvana. Asceticism and the vain upholding of precepts, vain meditation, and vain wisdom of non-Buddhists are not. Why? In Buddhism, it is by simultaneously practicing the three elements—namely, precepts, meditation, and wisdom—that one can enter nirvana. Just as a person who stands on level ground and holds a good bow and arrow can shoot an enemy to death, so do the three elements go together. Precepts are the level ground, meditation is a good bow, and wisdom a sharp arrow. When the three elements are complete, one can kill the enemy of defilements. For this reason, non-Buddhists cannot attain nirvana.

The practitioner at that time observes conditions in four aspects, like shooting [arrows]. He observes suffering in the [following] four aspects. Since [suffering] arises based on causes and conditions, it is [observed as] impermanent. Since [suffering] afflicts body and mind, it is [observed as] suffering. Since there is not a single thing that is perceivable, it is [observed as] empty. Since there is no action and no reception, it is [observed as being] without self. He observes the origin in the [following] four aspects. Since defilements and defiled karma come together, [the origin is observed as] collection. Since similar fruits arise, [it is observed as] a cause. Since all conditioned elements are perceived here, [it is observed as] arising. Since dissimilar fruits continue, [it is observed as] a condition. He observes the extinction [of suffering] in the [following] four aspects. Since [the extinction] covers up all defilements, it is [observed as] closure. Since it removes the fire of defilements, it is [observed as] cessation. Since it is the best among all elements, it is [observed as] superb. Since it goes beyond the world, it is [observed as] the exit. He observes the path in the [following] four aspects. Since it can reach nirvana, it is [observed as] the path. Since it is not perverted, it is [observed as] correct. Since it is the place where all awakened sages go, it is [observed as] footsteps. Since it can be freed from worldly agonies, it is [observed as] separation.

Those who thus observe attain the semblance of undefiled elements. [That] is called the stage of heat. Why is it called heat? Since one always practices diligently, it is called the stage of heat. Defilements are firewood, and undefiled wisdom is fire. When the burning fire [of wisdom] is about to break out, its first foreshadowing is called the stage of heat. It is just like the smoke that emerges first when one starts a fire. This is called "heat." This is the first sign of the path to nirvana.

Among the disciples of the Buddha, there are two types. One is those who like single-mindedness and seek meditation. They follow the defiled path.[43] The other is those who remove attachment and like true wisdom. They go directly to nirvana. Among those who enter the stage of heat, those who have the sign of heat attain single-mindedness [more] fundamentally. A mirror [that reflects] the true Dharma approaches the undefiled realm. *(A mirror image resembles the face, but [the face] does not exist within the mirror; therefore [a mirror] is mentioned as a simile.)* The practitioner at that time attains great peace. He thinks to himself: "I must definitely attain nirvana, because I have seen this path." It is like a man who while digging a well finds wet mud, and knows that he will attain water before long. It is like a man who defeats his enemies, and whose enemies have already withdrawn. Then he knows that he has attained victory and is peaceful in his mind. It is like a man who is suspected to be dead. People want to know if he is still alive. They should first examine him by beating his body with a stick. If hidden spots and veins appear, they know that there is still heat and he can definitely revive. It is also like a person who listens to the Dharma, reflects on it, rejoices, and whose mind is fixed. At that time, his mind gets heated. Since the practitioner has these types of heated elements, he is said to be heated and is said to be able to attain the roots of merit leading to nirvana. The elements

279c

53

of these roots of merit have the sixteen aspects of the Four [Noble] Truths as their objects. In the six stages, one wisdom becomes the basis for all undefiled elements. A wild person can go peacefully. *(Because he is apart from the undefiled, he is called a "wild person." Checking the Sanskrit text,*[44] *the former translation "unawakened people"* [lit., "common people"] *is not appropriate.)* This is called the element of heat.

When he goes further and makes progress, [the next stage] is called the summit stage. It is just like yogurt made from milk. This man observes the reality of [all] elements. "I shall attain deliverance from suffering. My mind loves this Dharma. This is the true Dharma that can remove various suffering, old age, sickness, and death." At that time, he thinks about who taught this Dharma. It was taught by the Buddha, the Blessed One. Thence he attains purified faith and great joy in the Buddha Jewel. "If it were not for this Dharma, who would be able to block all defilements? How would I attain true wisdom and a little illumination?" Thence he attains purified faith and great joy in the Dharma Jewel. "If I did not have good co-practitioners who are disciples of the Buddha, how would I attain true wisdom and a little illumination?" Thence he attains purified faith and great joy in the Sangha Jewel. Thus he attains purified single-mindedness in the Three Jewels and is united with true wisdom. These are the roots of merit of the summit and are also called the summit elements. They are also called the roots of merit that enable the attainment of nirvana. As is told in the *Pārāyana-sūtra:*

> The Buddha Jewel, Dharma [Jewel,] and Sangha Jewel. Those who have small purified faith [in them] are called [people who have attained] the roots of merit of the summit. You should uphold [these roots of merit] single-mindedly.

Why does [the verse] mention "small faith"? For the Buddha, bodhisattvas, solitary awakened ones (*pratyekabuddha*s), and arhats, [faith] is small, but for wild people [faith] is large. Further, this [faith] can be destroyed and lost, and so it is said to be "small." As is said in the *Dhammapada:*

> A plantain tree dies when it bears fruit, so does a bamboo when it bears fruit. A mule dies when it gives birth to a foal. A petty man dies when he gains profit.[45]

Because [honor] is destructive and is not profitable, when a petty man attains honor, his merits will be entirely exhausted, and he will fall from the elements of the summit.[46]

Also, [the practitioner] has not severed the binding defilements and has not attained the undefiled, boundlessly wise mind. For this reason, [faith] is said to be "small." Further, when [the practitioner] diligently practices single-mindedness and enters the path to nirvana, he observes the five aggregates and the sixteen aspects of the Four [Noble] Truths even more clearly. Then the mind does not shrink back, regret, or withdraw but wishes to enter [the stage of] recognition. This is called the roots of the merit of recognition. What does recognition refer to? The practice in accordance with the [sixteen] aspects of the Four [Noble] Truths is called recognition. These roots 280a of merit are classified into three classes, namely the advanced, intermediate, and low stages. What is called recognition? [The practitioner] observes the five aggregates as impermanent, painful, empty, and without self. [His] mind recognizes [this] and does not withdraw, and it is called recognition. Also he observes the world as entirely painful, empty, and without pleasure. This is [the truth of] suffering. Lust and other defilements as the cause [of suffering], these are [the truth of] cause. Extinction conditioned by wisdom, this is called the high[est] element, [which] nothing surpasses. The eightfold straight path can lead the practitioner to nirvana, and nothing surpasses [this path]. [He] thus believes and recognizes without regret or doubt. This is called recognition. In it there are still other [kinds of] recognition. Various bonds, defilements, doubts, and regret come into the mind but cannot destroy it. It is just like a rock mountain that cannot be moved by various winds or water. For this reason, it is called recognition. Thus [the practitioner] is called a truly good "wild person," as is told in the *Dhammapada* by the Buddha:

One who has attained much of the worldly correct view never falls into bad destinies even for ten million years.

This worldly correct view is called the roots of merit of recognition. This person greatly advances in single-mindedness and strongly abhors worldly phenomena. He wishes to clearly realize the [sixteen] aspects of the Four [Noble] Truths and go to nirvana. He is thus single-minded, and this is called the supreme among the worldly elements.

Simultaneously fixed on the four aspects—impermanence, suffering, emptiness, and no-self—[the practitioner's mind] observes one truth [of suffering], because the recognition of the elements of suffering [at the first moment of awakening] recognizes suffering. For what reason? [It is because the practitioner at that time] observes the impermanence, suffering, emptiness, and no-self of the five appropriated aggregates belonging to the realm of desire. Then mental recognition is subsumed under wisdom, and the mind and mental functions associated with it are also referred to as the recognition of the elements of suffering. Physical and verbal karma, as well as the conditioned elements not associated with the mind,[47] [also contribute to this recognition of the elements of suffering].

The first gate to all pure elements in the present and future is called the recognition of the elements of suffering. *("Elements" [refers to] pure elements. "Recognition" means faithful acceptance.)* It gives rise to the wisdom of the elements of suffering in the subsequent [moment]. The recognition of the elements of suffering severs binding defilements, and the wisdom of the elements of suffering [constitutes] realization [of the truth]. It is as if a person reaped [crops] and another tied them, or as if [a person] cut bamboo trees with a sharp knife and a wind knocked them down [to the ground]. Due to the exercise of recognition and wisdom, one can realize the above (i.e., severing the binding defilements and realizing the truth). One can sever the ten binding defilements belonging to the realm of desire that are to be severed by seeing [the truth of] suffering. Then [the practitioner] attains a pure wisdom that is different from worldly wisdom, even though he has not attained the acquisition[48] of pure wisdom. Then [the practitioner] attains one type of wisdom. *(Worldly wisdom will be attained later.)*

In the second moment of mind, [the practitioner] accomplishes the wisdom of elements, the wisdom of suffering, and worldly wisdom. Through the third and fourth moments of mind, he accomplishes four types of wisdom: the wisdom of suffering, the wisdom of elements, the wisdom of analogy, and worldly wisdom. In the wisdom of the elements of the [truth of] origin, extinction, and the path, respectively, one type of wisdom is added.[49] For people freed from desire, the accomplishment of mind-reading wisdom is added.[50] The analogical recognition of suffering and the analogical wisdom of suffering sever eighteen binding defilements. These four [moments of] mind are attained [while one realizes] the truth of suffering.

The recognition of the elements of origin and the wisdom of the elements of origin sever seven binding defilements belonging to the realm of desire. The analogical recognition of origin and the analogical wisdom of origin sever thirteen binding defilements belonging to the realm of form (*rūpadhātu*) and to the realm without form (*ārūpyadhātu*). 280b

The recognition of the elements of extinction and the wisdom of the elements of extinction sever seven binding defilements belonging to the realm of desire. The analogical recognition of extinction and the analogical wisdom of extinction sever twelve binding defilements belonging to the realm of form and to the realm without form.

The recognition of the elements of the path and the wisdom of the elements of the path sever eight binding defilements belonging to the realm of desire. The analogical recognition of the path and the analogical wisdom of the path sever fourteen binding defilements belonging to the realm of form and the realm without form.

The analogical wisdom of the path is called *srotāpanna (which means "flowing into nirvana"* ["stream-entrant"] *in Chinese)*. [Thus the practitioner] truly knows the nature of [all] elements [through these] sixteen moments of mind. During the [first] fifteen moments of mind, competent ones are referred to as "those who practice according to the teaching," and incompetent ones are referred to as "those who practice according to faith." If these two [types of practitioners] had not been freed [from any mental defilements before entering the Way of Seeing], they are called "those who are heading for the first fruit" [during the first fifteen moments of mind]. [When those] who had not severed binding defilements have attained the sixteen[th moment of] mind, they are called *srotāpanna* ("stream-entrant"). If they had severed six classes of binding defilements,[51] at the sixteen[th moment] of mind they are called *sakṛdāgāmin (which means "once-returner" in Chinese)*. If they had severed nine classes of binding defilemenents, at the sixteen[th moment] of mind they are called *anāgāmin (which means "non-returner" in Chinese)*. If those who had not been freed from desire before sever the eighty-eight binding defilements, they are called *srotāpanna*. Also, they acquire the roots of merit of undefiled fruits. Because of the acquisition [of these roots of merit], they are called *srotāpanna*. Competent ones are called "those who have attained [the truth] through seeing," and incompetent ones are called "those who are convinced [of the truth] through faith" [in the sixteenth moment].

Those who have not severed the binding defilements [to be severed through the path of repeated] contemplation have seven lifetimes to live. If they have severed the three classes of binding defilements [to be severed through the path of repeated] contemplation, they are called "those who are to be reborn in various families," who have three lifetimes to live. The eightfold noble path and the thirty-seven elements [conducive to awakening] are called the "stream." The stream [flows] toward nirvana, and since [the practitioner] follows the stream, he is called *srotāpanna*. He is considered to be the first meritorious son of the Buddha, [and as such the practitioner] can be liberated from bad destinies.

[When practitioners] have severed the three binding defilements and have attenuated the three poisons, they are called *sakṛdāgāmin*s ("once-returners"). Next, the nine classes of binding defilements belonging to the realm of desire *(top-top, top-middle, top-bottom, middle-top, middle-middle, middle-bottom, bottom-top, bottom-middle, and bottom-bottom)* [are classified into those] to be severed by seeing the [Four Noble] Truths, and [those] to be severed through [repeated] contemplation.

If unawakened people[52] had beforehand severed the [first] six classes of binding defilements belonging to the realm of desire by means of the defiled path and [then] enter the Way of Seeing the [Four Noble] Truths, at the sixteen[th moment of] mind, they attain the title *sakṛdāgāmin* ("once-returner"). If they had severed the [first] eight classes [of binding defilements belonging to the realm of desire] and enter the Way of Seeing the [Four Noble] Truths, at the sixteenth moment of mind one type [of them] is called [those who have attained] the fruit of *sakṛdāgāmin* ("once-returner") and are heading for *anāgāmin* ("non-returner"). If a disciple of the Buddha has attained *srotāpanna* ("stream-entrant"), by merely severing the three [classes of] binding defilements he is going to attain *sakṛdāgāmin* ("once-returner"). If he has severed the [first] six out of the nine types of binding defilements belonging to the realm of desire, he is called *sakṛdāgāmin* ("once-returner"). [If he has] severed the [first] eight types [of binding defilements], he is called a type of [practitioner who has attained] the fruit of *sakṛdāgāmin* ("once-returner") and is heading for *anāgāmin* ("non-returner").

If unawakened people had beforehand severed the nine classes of binding defilements belonging to the realm of desire and enter the Way of Seeing the [Four Noble] Truths, at the sixteen[th moment of] mind, they [come to be] called *anāgāmin*s ("non-returners").[53] If they have attained *sakṛdāgāmin* and further sever the [last] three classes of binding defilements [belonging to the realm of desire] to be severed by repeated contemplation, [at the moment of] the path of deliverance [severing] the ninth [class of binding defilements belonging to the realm of desire] they are called *anāgāmin*.[55] *Anāgāmin*s are of nine types: (1) *anāgāmin*s who definitely enter nirvana in this lifetime, (2) *anāgāmin*s who enter nirvana during the intermediate period [between this and next lifetimes], (3) *anāgāmin*s who enter nirvana after being born [in the next lifetime], (4) *anāgāmin*s who seek to enter nirvana with diligent practice, (5) *anāgāmin*s who seek to enter nirvana without diligent practice, (6) *anāgāmin*s who move upward [to higher realms of existence] and enter nirvana, (7) *anāgāmin*s who reach the [realm of] Akaniṣṭha and enter nirvana, (8) *anāgāmin*s who attain the absorption into the realm without form and enter nirvana, and (9) *anāgāmin*s who have attained [the absorption into cessation] with the body.

280c

*Anāgāmin*s heading for arhatship sever the [ninth] class of binding defilements belonging to the realm of form and realm without form with the unhindered path [that severs] the ninth [class of binding defilements, namely] the adamantine concentration that can destroy all binding defilements.[54]

The wisdom of extinction in the path of deliverance [that severs] the ninth [class of binding defilements] cultivates all roots of merit, and it is called the fruit of arhat. Arhats are of nine types: (1) Those who retrogress, (2) those who do not retrogress, (3) those who [consider] dying, (4) those who keep [their attainments], (5) those who stay [in the attained stage], (6) those who necessarily attain knowledge, (7) those whose [deliverance] is indestructible, (8) those who [attain] deliverance through wisdom, and (9) those who [attain] deliverance through both [wisdom and meditation].

(1) Those who are slow in their intellect and progress, and who retrogress by encountering five conditions: they are called "those who retrogress." (2) Those who are keen in their intellect and progress, and who do not retrogress

even though encountering five conditions: they are called "those who do not retrogress." (3) Those who are slow in their intellect and progress, but who are keen in their aversion [to the mundane world and] consider killing themselves [for fear of retrogressing from his attainment]: they are called "those who [consider] dying." (4) Those who are slow in their intellect but make great progress and protect themselves: they are called "those who keep [their attainment]." (5) Those who are average in their intellect and attainment, and who do not progress or regress and stay at the stage [they have attained]: they are called "those who stay [in the attained stage]." (6) Those who have somewhat keen intellect, make diligent effort, and can attain indestructible deliverance of mind: they are called "those who necessarily attain knowledge." (7) Those who have keen intellect, make great progress, and only then attain indestructible deliverance of mind: they are called "those whose [deliverance] is indestructible." (8) Those who cannot attain any [stages of] meditation but exhaust defilements while they have not attained meditation: they are called "those who [attain] deliverance through wisdom." (9) Those who attain various [stages of] meditation and the meditation of extinction and [thus] exhaust defilements: they are called "those who [attain] deliverance through both [wisdom and meditation]."

There are arhats who are always filled with aversion to all conditioned elements, do not seek further merit, and, when the proper time comes, enter nirvana. There are arhats who seek the four stages of meditation, four formless concentrations, four balanced minds, eight types of deliverance, eight superior realms, ten universal realms, nine successive [stages of meditation], six supernatural powers, wisdom from vows, *araṇī-samādhi (In Chinese, it means "disputelessness." Araṇī is [also] taken as "eventlessness" or "emptiness." A former translation says that Subhūti always practiced the practice of emptiness, but this is wrong. This must merely be the practice of disputelessness. Disputelessness merely means protecting sentient beings so that they do not dispute with [the practitioner] himself. "Dispute" is like Śāriputra and Maudgalyāyana's staying overnight at a potter's house and inducing Kokālika to dispute [with them])*, concentration that skips [intermediate stages], mixed meditation, the three gates to deliverance, and relinquishment, *(Relinquishment refers to the three gates to deliverance, namely, emptiness, wishlessness, and marklessness. Emptiness, wishlessness, and marklessness correspond to the twelve gates of mindfulness that remedy those who are attached to something.)* and further make diligent efforts with keen wisdom and enter these [types of] meritorious meditation. This means that [these arhats] have become "those who do not retrogress" and "those whose [deliverance] is indestructible."

When no buddha appears in the world, and when there is no Buddha-Dharma and no disciples [of the Buddha], people freed from desire appear [as] solitary awakened ones. Solitary awakened ones are of three levels: high, middle, and low.

Low[-level] ones are those who formerly attained *srotāpanna* or *sakṛdāgāmin*. This *srotāpanna* is born in the seventh lifetime among humankind, when there is no Buddha-Dharma, so that he cannot become [the Buddha's] disciple. He cannot be born into the eighth lifetime either.[56] In that case he becomes a solitary awakened one. If a *sakṛdāgāmin* is born in the second lifetime when there is no Buddha-Dharma, he cannot become [the Buddha's] disciple. He cannot be born into the third lifetime either. In that case he becomes a solitary awakened one.

There are people who wish to become solitary awakened ones. When they have planted the seeds of merit [for becoming] solitary awakened ones, and when [on the other hand their] merit [respective to the] Buddha-Dharma does not mature, they get weary of the world, become recluses, and attain awakening. They are called solitary awakened ones. They are middle[-level] solitary awakened ones.

There are people who seek the full awakening of the buddhas but whose power of wisdom and power to progress are only small. They retrogress because of certain causes and conditions *(like Śāriputra)*. At that time a buddha does not appear in the world, there is no Buddha-Dharma or [his] disciples, [but] their practice of [cultivating] the roots of merit matures and they become solitary awakened ones. Endowed with many or a few of the major and minor bodily marks [of a buddha], they grow weary of the world, become recluses, and attain awakening. They are called high[-level] solitary awakened ones.

Those who attain shallow wisdom of elements are called arhats. Those who attain moderate wisdom are called solitary awakened ones, and those

281a

who attain profound wisdom are called buddhas. It is like a person who looks at a tree from afar and cannot recognize branches. If he comes a little closer, he can recognize branches but cannot recognize flowers or leaves. When he has reached the bottom of the tree, he can recognize all the branches, leaves, flowers, and fruits of the tree.

Auditors (*śrāvaka*s) understand that all conditioned elements are impermanent, that all elements have no proprietor, and that only nirvana is good and peaceful. Auditors can observe [the conditioned elements] in this fashion, but they cannot analyze them, nor can they penetrate or understand them deeply. Solitary awakened ones can analyze them to some extent, but they also cannot penetrate or understand them deeply. Buddhas know elements and completely analyze them. They deeply penetrate and understand them.

It is like the king of Vārāṇasī who in a hot summer ascended his seat of seven jewels at the top floor of an elevated palace. He had a blue-dressed [servant girl] grind *gośīrṣa* sandalwood [into powder] and smear it on his body. The blue-dressed [servant girl] wore many bracelets on her arms, so when she smeared [the sandal powder] on the king's body, the bracelets made noises and filled the [king's] ears, irritating him greatly. [Therefore] the king told [the servant girl] to remove [the bracelets], and the fewer bracelets [she wore], the smaller the noise became. When she had only one bracelet on, there was no noise at all. Then the king realized [the truth] and said: "[If I have] many things, [namely] the state, subjects, courtiers, and court maidens, I shall have many worries in the same way." Instantly he became detached, meditated in a solitary place, and became a solitary awakened one. His hair and beard naturally dropped off, and he wore a natural robe. Leaving the elevated palace, by the power of miraculous movement, he became a recluse and entered a mountain. Such is the background of a middle-level solitary awakened one.

[Calling the Buddha to Mind]

If the practitioner seeks the full awakening of the buddhas, in meditation he should first fix his mind and concentrate on the living bodies of the buddhas in the ten directions and of the three periods of time. Do not call to mind [the elements of] earth, water, fire, wind; mountains, trees, grasses, or woods.

Do not call to mind anything with form between heaven and earth, or any other elements. Only call to mind the living bodies of buddhas staying in the air (lit., space). [One's visualized image of the Buddha should be] like Sumeru, the king of gold mountains, at the center of the pure water of the ocean. It is like a great fire burning in a dark night, or like a banner of seven jewels in a great shrine. The body of the Buddha is likewise; it has the thirty-two major and eighty minor bodily marks, which always emit boundless pure rays of light into the blue color that has the characteristics of space. [If the practitioner] always calls the bodily marks of the Buddha to mind in the way described above, the practitioner attains the concentration in which all the buddhas in the ten directions over the three periods appear in front of the mental eye, and in which he sees all of them. If the mind is distracted, he concentrates it and [again] calls the body of the Buddha to mind.   281b

At that time, the practitioner sees thirty trillion types of boundless buddhas in the east. Likewise in the south, west, north, the four subdirections, above, and below—in every direction [where the practitioner] puts his mind, he sees all [its] buddhas. It is like a man who looks at constellations at night, and who sees all of the hundreds of thousands of boundless sorts of constellations. When a bodhisattva has attained this concentration, he attenuates grave transgressions accumulated through boundless eons and removes minor transgressions.

Having attained this concentration, [the practitioner] should call to mind the Buddha's manifold and boundless virtues, namely, all the wisdom, understanding, insights, and virtues. [The Buddha] has attained great friendliness, great compassion, and freedom. He was the first to escape the shell of ignorance, [and he attained] the four types of fearlessness, five eyes, ten powers, and eighteen distinctive features. He can remove boundless suffering, save [beings] from the fear of old age and death, and give nirvana that is the eternal peace. The Buddha has these sorts of manifold and boundless virtues.

Having thought thus, [the practitioner] himself makes a wish and says: "(1) I shall one day attain a buddha's body whose merits are as stately as this." Then he makes a great vow: "(2) With all my merits in the past and present, I shall seek for the full awakening of the buddhas and shall not seek for other rewards." He further thinks as follows: "All sentient beings are truly pitiable. The meritorious bodies of buddhas are as stately as this. Why do sentient beings seek other karma and do not seek buddhahood? It is just like a blind son of a noble family who has fallen into a deep pit and, pressed by hunger, eats dung or mud. The father greatly pities for him and creates a means to save him from the deep pit and serves a superb meal for him." The practitioner thinks thus: (3) "Likewise is the ambrosia of the merit of the twofold bodies of buddhas. Sentient beings, however, have fallen into the deep pit of samsara and eat various impurities. With great compassion I will save all sentient beings and make them attain the full awakening of the buddhas and reach the [other] shore of [the river of] samsara. Thus I shall satisfy them with the Dharma taste of various merits. I wish that they may attain the entirety of the Buddha-Dharma. Listening, chanting, memorizing, questioning, practicing meditation, and attaining fruits are the steps [to buddhahood]. I shall make great essential vows and wear the armor of the three vows.[57] Outside I shall defeat a host of demons, and inside I shall smash the rogues of binding defilements. I shall enter [the path] straight and shall not make a detour. If one compares these three vows with innumerable [other] vows, [all] vows are included in these [three], because [these three] save sentient beings and let them attain the full awakening of the buddhas." Thus he thinks, and thus he wishes. This is called the bodhisattvas' concentration on calling buddhas to mind.

[Meditation on the Impurities]

[If] lust is predominant among the three poisons in a practitioner of the bodhisattva path, he should first observe the body. [The body is filled with such impurities as] bones, flesh, skin, tendons, vessels, flowing blood, liver, lungs, intestines, stomach, feces, urine, tears, and saliva. [Thus he observes] the impurity of the thirty-six items [in his body] and the nine images [of the decomposition of a corpse]. He devotes his mind to the inner contemplation without letting his mind be distracted by other objects. If his mind is distracted, he concentrates it and returns it [to the original objects of meditation]. It is just like a person who enters a granary holding a torch and recognizes beans, barley, Chinese millet, and foxtail millet, without omitting anything.

281c

Then [the practitioner] analyzes the body into the six elements. Hardness is the earth element. Moisture is the water element. Heat is the fire element. Movement is the wind element. Cavity is the space element. Perception is the consciousness element. It is also like butchering a cow and cutting it into six portions, with the trunk, head, and four limbs placed separately.

The body has nine apertures that are always leaking impurities. [It is also like] a leather bag full of feces. He always makes this contemplation without letting his mind be distracted by other objects. If his mind is distracted, he concentrates it and returns it [to the original objects of meditation]. If [the practitioner] attains single-mindedness, he develops aversion in his mind, seeks to be liberated from his body, and wants to annihilate it quickly and soon enter nirvana. Then he should arouse great friendliness and compassion. [In order to] save sentient beings with [his] great merit, he makes the aforementioned three vows. "Since sentient beings do not realize impurities, they create pollution through various transgressions. I shall save them [from the flood of samsara] and place them on the ground of ambrosia. Further, sentient beings in the realm of desire are attached to impurities like dogs eating feces. I should save them and lead them to the pure path.

"Then I should seek for the reality of [all] elements, which is neither permanent nor impermanent, or neither pure nor impure. How could I insist that they are impure? The wisdom that observes impurity arises from causes and conditions. If I follow our Dharma, I should seek reality. How can I [learn to] detest the impurities in my body and attain nirvana? Like a great elephant that crosses a rapid stream [with its feet] on the bottom, I should attain the reality of [all] elements and enter nirvana. How can I be like monkeys or rabbits that fear the rapid stream and hasten to save themselves? I should now learn that, according to the bodhisattva Dharma, practicing meditation on the impurities and removing lust is [done in order] to teach sentient beings widely and detach them from the misfortunes caused by lust. I should not be overwhelmed by meditation on the impurities."

Further, since one has already observed the impurities and detests samsara, one should observe the pure aspects. One ties one's mind to the three spots: the tip of the nose, the area between the brows, and the forehead. In the middle of these spots one should [cut] open the skin for one inch and remove blood and flesh. One then concentrates one's mind on the white bone without letting the mind be distracted by other objects. If the mind is distracted, one should concentrate it and return it [to the original objects of meditation].

While one is concentrated on the three objects, one constantly fights with one's mind. It is as if two people were wrestling together. If the practitioner [wants to] win over the mind, the best way is to control [the mind] and fix it. This is called "single-mindedness." If one gives rise to great compassion because of aversion [to the suffering of sentient beings], one takes pity on them, [thinking]: "For the sake of these empty bones, they stay away from nirvana and enter the three bad destinies.[58] I should exert myself to cultivate various merits, teach sentient beings, and make them understand that the characteristic of the body is empty. The bones are enveloped in the skin, but in fact [the body] is filled with impurities. For the sake of sentient beings, I shall little by little explain these characteristics of the elements."

If one considers [the body] as pure even a little, one's mind develops attachment. If one mostly thinks of the impurity [of the body], one's mind develops aversion. Because one goes beyond the characteristics of elements, the true Dharma emerges. In the reality of [all] elements, there is no purity or impurity, nor is there enclosure or exit. One sees the equality of elements; [the reality is] indestructible and immovable. This is called the reality of elements. *(Thus one goes beyond the Dharma of arhats.)*

282a

[Cultivation of Friendliness]

[If] anger is predominant in a practitioner of the bodhisattva path, he should practice friendly mind. He should call to mind the sentient beings in the east with pure friendly mind free from hatred or anger, and with vast and boundless [mind]. He sees various sentient beings all in front of him. He [then] likewise calls to mind [the beings] in the south, west, north, the four subdirections, above, and below. He controls his mind and practices friendliness without letting his mind be distracted by other objects. If his mind is distracted, he concentrates it and returns it [to the original objects of meditation]. He should look at all sentient beings with his mental eye clearly, as if they were just in front of him. If he attains single-mindedness, he should make a vow and say: "I shall liberate sentient beings and let them attain true happiness with the truly pure Dharma of nirvana." If he practices the concentration on friendliness, and if his mind is as stated above, this is the bodhisattva path.

Abiding in the concentration on friendliness, [such practitioners] observe the reality of [all] elements, which is pure, indestructible, and immovable. They wish to let sentient beings attain this benefit of the Dharma. With this concentration, in friendliness they call to mind all sentient beings in the east and let them attain the happiness of buddha[hood]. They do the same [with regard to

66

the sentient beings] in the ten directions. Their minds are not perverted. This is called the method of concentration on friendliness of bodhisattvas.

Question: Why do they not call to mind the sentient beings in the ten directions altogether at the same time?

Answer: It is easier to attain single-mindedness if they first call to mind [the sentient beings] in one direction. Afterward, they gradually extend [the objects of reflection] to the other directions.

Question: If a person has an enemy who always wants to harm him, how can he practice friendliness and want to let the enemy attain happiness?

Answer: Friendliness is a mental element and originates from the mind. First one should start with people one likes. Then people one likes are gradually expanded and finally they encompass enemies. When a fire burns wood, it can burn even wet [wood] if [the fire] is sufficiently large. The matter is the same here.

Question: Sometimes sentient beings encounter various [kinds of] suffering, among human beings or in the hells. Even if bodhisattvas are compassionate, how can [suffering] people attain happiness?

Answer: First they capture the image of happiness from happy people, and then let the suffering people attain that happiness. It is just like the terrified and disheartened commander of a defeated army who sees his enemies and thinks that they are all stout soldiers.

Question: What benefits does the practice of the concentration on friendliness have?

Answer: The practitioner himself thinks as follows: "Those who have become recluses and are detached from the secular world should practice friendliness." He further thinks: "Since I eat food donated by believers, I should practice [for their] benefit. As has been told by the Buddha: 'To practice friendliness even for a moment is to follow the teaching of the Buddha.' Thus I receive donations not in vain but to achieve awakening (lit., "enter the path"). Next, although the body wears a dyed robe, the mind should not be dyed. The power of the concentration on friendliness can make the mind spotless.[59] Then my mind practices friendliness. In the period of destroying the Dharma, I abide by the Dharma. Among the Dharma-less people, I abide by the Dharma. I follow the Dharma and do not harm [others]. Due to the power of the concentration on friendliness, bodhisattvas practice the path and go to the gate of ambrosia. The coolness of friendliness cools down various types of agonizing heat. As has been said by the Buddha, 'When one feels extreme heat, entering a cool pond is pleasant.'"

Next, wearing the armor of great friendliness, the practitioner guards himself from the arrows of defilements. Friendliness is the Dharma medicine that detoxifies the poison of hatred. Friendliness can remove the defilements that burn the mind. Friendliness is the stairway of Dharma by which to ascend 282b the tower of deliverance. Friendliness is the Dharma boat to cross over the sea of samsara. When seeking for the assets of good Dharma, friendliness is the utmost treasure. For traveling to nirvana, friendliness is the provisions of food for the way. Friendliness is the fine horse on which to enter nirvana. Friendliness is a valiant general who overcomes the three bad destinies. One who can practice friendliness can eradicate many evils. Various good deities follow and protect him.

Question: If a practitioner attains the concentration on friendliness, how can he not lose it but promote it?

Answer: Studying the precepts and [keeping them] pure. Good faith in [meditational] comfort and pleasure. Studying various [types of] meditation, single-mindedness, and wisdom. Wishing to be in a silent place. Always being attentive. Little desire and satisfaction. Behaviors conforming to the teachings of friendliness. Controlling oneself and eating little. Restricting sleep. Meditation in the first and last watches of night without cessation. Elimination of disturbing speech and maintaining silence. Knowing the time for rest while sitting, lying down, walking, and standing, and not exerting oneself excessively, to the point of exhaustion. Adjusting the temperature so that it is not disturbing. These [elements] promote friendliness.

Next, giving the pleasure of the full awakening of the buddhas and nirvana to all people is called great friendliness. The practitioner thinks: "Great people[60] in the present and future practice friendliness and benefit all. I also have benefited; this has been a good help for me. I shall also practice friendliness and repay my indebtedness." Further he thinks: "People of great virtue commiserate with all [sentient beings] with friendly minds and consider that a pleasure. I should be the same. [I shall] call those sentient beings to mind and let them achieve the happiness of [becoming] buddhas and [attaining] nirvana." This is the repayment of indebtedness.

Further, the power of friendliness makes their minds all attain pleasure, and it makes their bodies all free from agonizing heat, and [helps them] attain cool pleasure. Continuing to practice meritorious [deeds] of friendliness, [the practitioner] wishes to bring peace to all beings and thus repay his indebtedness to them.

Also, friendliness is profitable in the following ways. It severs the element of anger and opens the gate of reputation. [Friendliness] is a good field [of merit] for donors and is a cause for [subsequent] birth in the Brahmā Heaven. [Friendliness] resides in the realm of detachment and removes the roots of enmity and dispute. [Friendliness] is something that buddhas praise and wise people respect. [Friendliness] enables the observance of the pure precepts, brings about the light of wisdom, and makes listening to the benefits of the Dharma possible. [Friendliness] is the crème de la crème of merit, which determines [one's identity] as a good person. [Friendliness] is a great power for recluses and eliminates various evils. A friendly response can subdue the evil of abusive words. [Friendliness] accumulates joy and gives rise to the element of diligence. [Friendliness] is the root cause of wealth, a storehouse of practical wisdom, a repository of truthful faith, the gate to various good elements, the way to gain a [good] reputation, the root of reverence, and the true path of the buddhas.

If one maintains a bad [practice], one will experience its bad consequences oneself. There are five kinds of bad speech: untimely, untruthful, unbeneficial, unfriendly, and ungentle. These five kinds of bad speech cannot undermine [friendliness]. All [the types of] evil are also unable to harm [friendliness]. They are just like small fires that cannot heat up the great ocean. *(Below the text will tell the story of King Udayana having five hundred arrows.)*[61]

According to the *avadāna* (story) of King Udayana in the *Vīrasūtra*, [the king] had two consorts: one was Anupamā, the other Śyāmāvatī. Anupamā slandered Śyāmāvatī. Śyāmāvatī had five hundred honest people. The king wanted to kill them one by one by shooting five hundred arrows. Śyāmāvatī told [all] those honest people to stand behind her. Then Śyāmāvatī entered the concentration on friendliness. The king bent his bow and shot her, but the arrow fell at her feet. The second arrow turned back and [fell] at the king's feet. The king, in a panic, tried to shoot another arrow, but Śyāmāvatī said to him: "Stop it, stop it. Let us talk about the fidelity between husband and wife. If you shoot that arrow, it will straightway pierce your heart."

282c

In terror, the king then threw down his bow and gave up shooting. He asked [her]: "What magic have you mastered?" [She] answered: "I have no magic. This is merely because I, as a disciple of the Buddha, have entered the concentration on friendliness."

This concentration on friendliness, in sum, has three objects: sentient beings, elements, and nothingness. [The friendliness] of those who have not attained the path is directed to sentient beings. [That of] arhats and solitary awakened ones is directed to elements. [That of] buddhas, the Blessed Ones, is directed to nothingness.

Thus is the abridged exposition of the method of the concentration on friendliness.

[Observation of Dependent Origination]

[If] ignorance is predominant in a practitioner of the bodhisattva path, he should contemplate the twelve links [of dependent origination] and destroy the two kinds of ignorance. Inwardly they destroy ignorance about themselves, and outwardly they destroy ignorance about sentient beings.

They meditate as follows: "Sentient beings and myself are both in calamitous [situations]. Ever being born, ever growing old, ever becoming sick, ever dying, ever perishing, and ever departing, sentient beings pitiably do not know the way to escape [this situation]. How can they be liberated?"

[Bodhisattvas] contemplate single-mindedly that birth, old age, sickness, and death are caused by something. They should further contemplate what causes these [situations]. They contemplate single-mindedly, [as follows]: Birth is caused by existence, existence by grasping, grasping by craving, craving by sensation, sensation by contact, contact by the six realms of cognition, the six realms of cognition by "name" and form, "name" and form by consciousness, consciousness by conduct, and conduct by ignorance.

Likewise they further think: "What brings about the cessation of birth, old age, and death?" They contemplate single-mindedly, [as follows]: The cessation of old age and death is brought about by the cessation of birth, the cessation of birth by the cessation of existence, the cessation of existence by the cessation of grasping, the cessation of grasping by the cessation of craving, the cessation of craving by the cessation of sensation, the cessation of sensation by the cessation of contact, the cessation of contact by the cessation of the six realms of cognition, the cessation of the six realms of cognition by the cessation of "name" and form, the cessation of "name" and form by the cessation of consciousness, the cessation of consciousness by the cessation of conduct, the cessation of conduct by the cessation of consciousness, and the cessation of conduct by the cessation of ignorance.

Here, what are the twelve links? The link of ignorance means not knowing the anterior, not knowing the posterior, not knowing the anterior or posterior, not knowing the interior, not knowing the exterior, not knowing the interior or exterior, not knowing the Buddha, not knowing the Dharma, not knowing the Sangha, not knowing suffering, not knowing its origin, not knowing its extinction, not knowing the path, not knowing karma, not knowing its fruit, not knowing karma or its fruit, not knowing the cause, not knowing the condition, not knowing the cause or condition, not knowing transgressions, not knowing merits, not knowing transgressions or merits, not knowing the good, not knowing the evil, not knowing the good or evil, not knowing sinful elements, not knowing innocent elements, not knowing what should be approached, not knowing what should be alienated, not knowing defiled elements, not knowing undefiled elements, not knowing mundane elements, not knowing supramundane elements, not knowing past elements, not knowing future elements, not knowing present elements, not knowing black elements, not knowing white elements, not knowing the way to analyze causes and conditions, now knowing the six tactile elements, and not knowing the realized elements. These various sorts of dark ignorance of not-knowing, not-understanding, and not-seeing are [all] called ignorance.

Ignorance causes conduct. What is conduct? There are three kinds of conduct: bodily conduct, oral conduct, and mental conduct.

What is bodily conduct? Inhalation and exhalation are the elements of bodily conduct. Why? Because these elements belong to the body, they are called bodily conduct.

What is oral conduct? [The elements that accompany] reflection and investigation. It is after reflection and investigation that one speaks. Without reflection and investigation, there is no speech. These [elements] are called oral conduct.

What is mental conduct? "Ache" and ideation *(People in the world are attached to the term "ache." [Since] there are three types of "aches,"[62] "ache"*

283a

should be retranslated as "sensation." Sensation corresponds to the realms of the world. Because one does not experience pain or pleasure in the upper realms,[63] *[the translation "ache" is improper.] One should say that sensation and ideation are annoyances for recluses.)* are mental elements, because they belong to the mind. Thus they are mental conduct. There is also conduct belonging to the realm of desire, the realm of form, and the realm without form. Further, there are [three types of] conduct: good, evil, and immovable. What is good conduct? All good conduct in the realm of desire and of the [lower] three stages of the realm of form.[64] What is evil conduct? Evil elements. What is immovable conduct? Defiled good conduct [belonging to the realm of] the fourth stage of meditation and defiled good conduct [belonging to the realms of] the immaterial absorptions.[65] These [elements] are called conduct.

Conduct causes consciousness. What is consciousness? There are six elements of consciousness: visual consciousness up to mental consciousness. They are called the six consciousnesses.

Consciousness causes "name" and form. What is "name"? The immaterial four elements, namely, "ache," ideation, conduct, and consciousness. These are called "name." What is "form"? All material four gross elements and composite matter. These are called "form."[66] What are the four gross elements? Earth, water, fire, and wind. What is earth? Those that are characterized by hardness are earth. Those that are characterized by moisture are water. Those that are characterized by heat are fire. Those that are characterized by light mobility are wind. The other material elements are easy to understand. Those that are tangible or intangible are called composite matter. The "names" and forms taken together, they are called "name" and form.[67]

"Names" and form cause the six realms of cognition. What are the six realms of cognition? There are six internal realms: the visual internal realm up to the mental internal realm. They are called the six realms of cognition.

The six realms of cognition condition contact. What is contact? There are six elements of contact: visual contact up to mental contact. What is visual contact? The eye conditioned by a piece of matter gives rise to the visual consciousness.[68] The meeting of these three elements is called visual contact. [The other types of contact] up to the mental contact are defined in the same way.

Contact causes sensation. What is sensation? There are three types of sensation: pleasant sensation, painful sensation, and neutral sensation. What is pleasant sensation? The defilement of desire. What is painful sensation? The defilement of anger. What is neutral sensation? The defilement of ignorance. Further, pleasant sensation is pleasant when it arises and stays, but painful when it ceases. Painful sensation is painful when it arises and stays, but pleasant when it ceases. Neutral sensation is not perceived as either painful or pleasant.

283b

Sensation causes craving. What is craving? The craving induced by the contact of the eye and visible objects, up to the craving induced by the contact of the mind and concepts.

Craving causes grasping. What is grasping? Grasping [the objects of] desire, grasping [wrong] views, grasping [wrong] precepts, and grasping the concept of self.

Grasping causes existence. What is existence? There are three kinds of existence. Existence [in the realm] of desire, existence [in the realm] of form, and existence [in the realm] without form. From the Avīci Great Hell below up to the heaven where one can enjoy the supernatural creations of other deities above,[69] as well as the karma that brings about rebirth in these [realms], are called existence [in the realm] of desire.[70] What is existence [in the realm] of form? From the Brahmā World below up to Akaniṣṭha Heaven, these are called existence [in the realm] of form. What is the existence [in the realm] without form? From [the realm of boundless] space up to the realm neither with nor without ideation, these are called existence [in the realm] without form.

Existence causes birth. What is birth? Various sentient beings are born in their respective realms and attain the appropriated aggregates, constituent elements, realms of cognition, and life. These are called birth.

Birth causes old age and death. What is old age? Lost teeth, gray hair, and many wrinkles. Sense organs become [over]mature and dysfunctional. The vital energy is blocked. The body becomes crooked, and one leans on a stick when walking. The body made of aggregates becomes decrepit. These are called old age.

What is death? The fall, perishing, discontinuation, loss of life force, and exhaustion of life of all sentient beings in respective realms. These are called death.

One first gets old and then dies, and therefore [this whole process] is called old age and death.

Here are the twelve links of dependent origination. Nothing in this world arises without cause or [due to] a deity, [any particular] human being, or various wrong conditions. When bodhisattvas observe the twelve links of dependent origination, they fix their minds fast, without letting their minds be distracted by other objects. If their minds are distracted, they concentrate their minds and return them [to the objects of meditation]. Thus they observe the twelve links and birth in the three periods: the previous birth, the present birth, and the next birth.

If a bodhisattva attains a fixed mind, he should observe that the twelve links are empty and without a proprietor. Ignorance does not perceive that it creates conduct. Conduct does not perceive that it has arisen from ignorance. Conduct simply arises conditioned by ignorance. It is just like a sprout arising from the seed of a plant. The seed does not perceive that it produces the sprout. Nor does the sprout perceive that it has arisen from the seed. Likewise up to old age and death. [The bodhisattva] observes and realizes that each of these twelve links has neither proprietor nor self. It is just like plants of the external [world] that have no proprietor. Merely out of wrong views one misconceives that there is self.

Question: If there is no self, no proprietor, and no function, why do [people] say "to leave [from one lifetime]" and "to come [to another lifetime," namely] to die here and to be born there?

Answer: Although there is no self, the six sense organs as cause and the six sense objects as condition give rise to the six consciousnesses. Because these three[71] come together, the element of contact arises, and one perceives various karmic [phenomena]. Thus, [people] say "to leave" and "to go," and accordingly, there are birth and death.

It is just like a lens, which, as a cause, brings about fire when it is placed near sundried cow dung. Likewise are the five aggregates. Because the five aggregates in this life arise, those in the next life emerge. It is not that the five aggregates in this life continue until the next life. At the same time, the five aggregates in the next life are attained not without connection to those in this life. The five aggregates just emerge from [their] causes and conditions, just like a sprout that emerges out of a seed of grain. This seed does not appear at the sprout or at another sprout.[72] [The seed and sprout are] neither different nor the same. Likewise is the attainment of the body of the next life.

283c

It is just like a tree that does not yet have a trunk, joints, branches, leaves, flowers, or fruit. When the right time comes, flowers and leaves become complete. Retribution for good and bad deeds [occur] in the same way. Because seeds perish, [the seeds and sprouts are] not eternal or identical. Because sprouts, stem, leaves and so forth grow, [the seeds and sprouts are] not separate or different. The succession of death and birth is also the same.

The practitioner knows that the various elements are impermanent, painful, empty, without self, and naturally arising and ceasing. He knows that [their] cause is such elements[73] as craving, that the extinction of the cause is cessation, and that the way leading to cessation is the path. Knowing the twelve links with these four types of wisdom is the correct Way of Seeing. Sentient beings are deceived by [mental] bondage, like a person who has a priceless jewel but does not recognize that it is a real [jewel] and is deceived by other people. At that time the bodhisattva generates a truly compassionate mind [and makes the following resolve]: "I will become a buddha and teach the true Dharma to those sentient beings, making them see the correct path."

Question: According to the Mahayana [Sutra on] the Perfection of Wisdom, correct view is [the understanding] that various elements do not arise or cease; that they are empty without entity; and that they have one characteristic, [namely] no characteristic. Why do you say that the meditation on impermanence and so forth is the correct view?

Answer: If Mahayana [scriptures] say that various elements are empty and have no characteristics, how can you say that impermanence, painfulness, emptiness, and so forth are untrue? If you say that non-arising, non-ceasing, and emptiness are real characteristics, you should not say "no characteristics." Your arguments are self-contradictory. Furthermore, the Buddha has taught [that there are] four perverted [views]. [The teaching that] taking impermanence for permanence is a perverted view is also reasonable. All conditioned elements are impermanent. Why? It is because they arise based on causes and conditions. Causes are impermanent, and so are conditions. How could the resultant fruit be permanent? What did not exist before now exists. Having existed, it will no longer exist. All sentient beings see impermanence. Inside there are old age, sickness, and death. Everything outside is seen to decline. How can you say that impermanence is unreal?

Question: I am not saying that permanence is real and impermanence is unreal. I am saying that permanence and impermanence are both unreal. Why? The Buddha said: "In emptiness, neither permanence nor impermanence can be perceived. If one is attached to these two sides, both of them are perverted [views]."

Answer: Your arguments do not agree with the Dharma. Why? If you say "no *dharma*,"[74] how can you say "both are perverted [views]" at the same time? That everything is empty without entity is true and is not perverted. If I reject permanence, I am attached to impermanence. The concept of self should be rejected, and there is no real self. In order to reject perverted [views] of permanence, one observes impermanence. Why? The power of impermanence can reject permanence, like one poison that can counteract another poison. It is just like a medicine that should be removed after healing a disease. One should know that a medicine is good because it can heal a disease. If the medicine is not removed, afterward the medicine itself will cause [another] disease. Here the matter is the same. If one becomes attached to the concept of impermanence, it should be rejected because it is not real. I have not accepted the concept of impermanence. How can I reject it?

284a

The Buddha said: "Suffering is the real suffering of the Four Noble Truths. Who could make it pleasant? The cause of suffering is the real cause. Who could make it a non-cause? The extinction of suffering is the real extinction. Who could make it non-extinction? The path leading to extinction is the real path. Who could make it a non-path? The sun might be made cold, the moon might be made hot, and wind might be made immovable, but these Four Noble Truths could never ever be made otherwise." You are unable to understand the Mahayana [teachings] and are merely attached to words. The reality of [all] elements that the Mahayana teaches is indestructible; it has no creator. If it were subject to destruction and creation, it would not be the Mahayana.

It is just like the moon that first emerges [at the beginning of the month]. When it emerges, the moon of the first or the second day is very thin. A person with keen eyes can find and show it to the one who has not found it. This person who has not found the moon might just look at the finger, unable to find the moon. The person with keen eyes says to him: "Stupid! Why are you just looking at my finger? The finger is the indicator of the moon; the finger is not the moon [itself]." You are also the same way. Words are not reality. They just provisionally express the real principle. You nonetheless are attached to words and are ignorant of reality. If the practitioner attains the aforementioned correct view, he observes the twelve links as a whole in their causal and resultant aspects. The twelve links in their resultant aspect are considered to be the truth of suffering. The twelve links in their causal aspect are considered to be the truth of origin. The extinction of the cause is the truth of extinction. Seeing the cessation of the causes and fruits is the truth of the path. There are four ways to observe the fruits: impermanence, suffering, emptiness, and no-self. There are four ways to observe the causes: origin, cause, condition, and arising.

Question: The fruits have four ways [to be observed], but they are merely called the truth of suffering. Do the other [three] (i.e., impermanence, emptiness, and no-self) have no name as truth?

Answer: Even if I say "the truth of impermanence," you will still have doubt. "The truth of suffering" and "the truth of no-self" will also be doubted, so that it would be difficult to subsume them under one [truth]. Further, even if one says "the truth of impermanence," there is no problem. "The truth of emptiness" and "the truth of no-self" do not have any problem either. If one says, "the truth of impermanence, suffering, emptiness, and no-self," it is redundant. Therefore the four aspects are subsumed under one [truth].

Question: By what distinguishing [characteristics] is only suffering used as the name [of the first truth], and not the other three?

Answer: Suffering is what all sentient beings detest and fear, not impermanence. Sometimes there are people who, oppressed by suffering, think of "attaining impermanence" (i.e., killing themselves). There is no one, however, who wants to attain suffering.

Question: There are people who want to hold swords and kill themselves, [who practice asceticism, like sitting on a mat of] needles or burning [themselves], [who take] bitter medicine, and [who] break into [other people's places and are punished later]. Are those kinds of people not seeking suffering?

Answer: [These acts are done] not for the sake of attaining suffering, but in the wish of keeping great pleasure. Because one fears suffering, one chooses death. Suffering is the greatest trouble, and pleasure is the greatest benefit. Therefore, escaping real suffering, one attains pleasure. For this reason, the Buddha calls [the twelve links in their] resultant aspects merely the truth of suffering, and not the truth of impermanence, emptiness, or no-self.

Thus, the wisdom of clear realization of these Four [Noble] Truths without any doubt or regret is called correct view.

284b

Thinking of these [Four Truths] more and more in various ways is called correct thought.

Subsuming the four kinds of correct speech, excluding the four kinds of wrong speech subsumed under wrong livelihood and the other four kinds of wrong speech, [is correct speech].[75]

[Conduct] excluding the three kinds of bodily conduct subsumed under wrong livelihood and the other three kinds of wrong conduct is called correct conduct.

[Livelihood] excluding various kinds of wrong livelihood is called correct livelihood.

When one meditates as above, one makes efforts. This is correct means.

Keeping these matters in mind without being distracted is called correct mindfulness.

Immovable meditation on these matters is called correct concentration.

The correct view is like a king, and the [other] seven elements follow.[76] These are called the truth of the path.

Single-minded and immovable belief in these matters is called the faculty of faith.

Single-minded and diligent pursuit of the path is called the faculty of diligence.

Single-minded mindfulness without obliviousness is called the faculty of mindfulness.

Fixing the mind on one point without letting one's mind be distracted by other objects is called the faculty of concentration.

Realization of impermanence and so forth by reflection and analysis is called the faculty of wisdom.

When these [five] faculties are enhanced, they are called the five powers.

Question: Wisdom, mindfulness, concentration, and so forth have been all explained under the heading of the eightfold correct path. Why are they explained again under the faculties and powers?

Answer: When one enters practice, one first attains small benefits. At that time they are called faculties. These five elements are promoted and become powerful, and then they are called powers. When one first enters the undefiled Way of Seeing the [Four Noble] Truths, these merits are called the eightfold correct path. When one enters the Way of Meditation, they are called the seven elements of awakening. When one first enters the Way, one is always single-mindedly aware of the body, "ache," mind, and concepts. [Then] they are called the four applications of mindfulness. [When] one thus attains the fine flavor of Dharma and makes four types of efforts, those [efforts] are called the four correct exertions. These wishes and exertions are the first step for concentration and wisdom. [When] one [further] diligently seeks autonomous control [of these elements], it is called the four supernatural powers.

Although [these types of practice] are called the four applications of mindfulness, four correct exertions, four supernatural powers, five faculties, and so forth, all [these types of practice] are done simultaneously. Different names are applied [only] according to one's progress, stage of practice, and [relative] intensity of practice. In the case of the four gross elements, each [element] has the four elements, but they are referred to according to the predominant element. If the constituent element of earth is predominant, and those of water, fire, and wind are subordinate, it is called the constituent element of earth. The same applies to the [constituent elements of] water, fire, and wind. In the same way, among the thirty-seven items [of practice], each item has various [other] items. For example, the four applications of mindfulness have the four right exertions, four supernatural powers, five faculties, five powers, seven [elements of] awakening, eightfold correct path, and so forth. If one thus observes the twelve links [of dependent origination], the practice on the Four [Noble] Truths, the four applications of mindfulness, four correct exertions, four supernatural powers, five faculties, five powers, seven [elements of] awakening, and eightfold correct path, one's mind becomes peaceful. One can also save sentient beings by these methods.

When one single-mindedly vows to seek buddhahood diligently, one thinks in one's mind as follows: "Although I see this path clearly, I should not attain realization [according to it]. Due to the following two reasons, I will not yet enter nirvana. First, [a bodhisattva with] great compassion does not forsake sentient beings. Second, I deeply understand the reality of [all]

284c

elements. Various minds and mental functions arise from causes and conditions [and are thus unreal]. How should I follow these unreal things? I will meditate on and enter into deep observation of the twelve links of dependent origination and know what they are." One further thinks: "There are four conditions: causal condition, successive condition, cognitive condition, and influential condition. Causal condition refers to the five conditions. Successive condition refers to the mind and mental functions in the past and present, other than the last moment of the mind of past and present arhats [which has no following moment]. Cognitive and influential conditions condition all elements."

One further thinks: "If we say that an element already exists in its causal condition, we cannot say that this element has arisen from the causal condition. If [an element] does not exist [in its causal condition], in that case we also cannot say that [the element] has arisen from the causal condition. [If an element] half exists and half does not exist [in its causal condition], in that case again we cannot say that [it] has arisen from the causal condition. How could there be a causal condition? If past mind and mental functions cease when the element has not yet arisen, how could [these past mind and mental functions] work as successive conditions? If refined elements[77] cannot be recognized according to the Buddhist teaching, how could nirvana be a cognitive condition?

If elements in fact have no intrinsic nature, there cannot be any existing elements. If fruits arise [based on] causes and conditions, [it means that] something exists caused by another thing. This argument is unacceptable. Whether [fruits on the one hand and] causes and conditions [on the other] are separate or together, these fruits cannot exist. How could fruits arise where there are causes and conditions, because there are no fruits in the causes and conditions? If fruits arise even though there have been no fruits in the causes and conditions before, why do fruits not arise where there are irrelevant causes and conditions? [I am raising this question] because both (i.e., relevant causes and conditions and irrelevant ones) are impossible. Fruits belong to causes and conditions and arise where causes and conditions exist. Their causes and conditions are not independent and belong to other causes and conditions. Thus these fruits would belong to other causes and conditions. How could dependent causes and conditions give rise to their fruits? Therefore, fruits do not arise from [either relevant] or irrelevant causes and conditions. Thus they are not fruits. Because there are no fruits, [relevant] or irrelevant conditions do not exist either.[78]

Question: The Buddha said that in the [scheme of the] twelve links of dependent origination, ignorance conditions conduct. How can you say that there are no causes or conditions?

Answer: I have already answered this above. You should not make further objections. If[, however,] you still have objections, I will give you an additional response. The Buddha said: "Erroneous recognition and unintelligence caused by the eye and conditioned by visible objects are ignorance." Here, depending on what does ignorance exist? Does it depend on the eye, visible objects, or consciousness? Ignorance should not depend on the eye. If ignorance depended on the eye, even without visible objects there would always be unintelligence. If ignorance depended on visible objects, the eye would not be necessary. [If so,] this would be external unintelligence without regard to oneself. [If ignorance] depended on consciousness, [since] consciousness, as well as ignorance, is immaterial, nonresistant, intangible, indivisible, and nonspatial, how could [ignorance] depend on [consciousness]?

For these reasons, ignorance is neither internal, nor external, nor intermediate. It does not come from the previous life, and it does not proceed to the next life. Nor does it come from the east, west, south, north, the four subdirections, above, or below. It is not a substantial element. Thus is the nature of ignorance.

If one realizes the nature of ignorance, it turns into intelligence. When one analyzes each [element], unintelligence is not perceived [anywhere]. How could ignorance condition conduct? Just like space that does not arise or cease, that does not exist or come to an end, and that is intrinsically pure, ignorance also does not arise or cease, does not exist or come to an end, and is intrinsically pure. Up to birth that conditions old age and death, the matter is the same. A bodhisattva thus observes the twelve links of dependent origination and knows that sentient beings are in delusion and entangled in misfortune. [He also knows] that [beings] are easy to save. If elements were substantial, [sentient beings] would be difficult to save. Thinking thus, [a bodhisattva] destroys ignorance.

285a

[Mindful Inhalation and Exhalation]

If discursive thoughts are predominant in a practitioner of the bodhisattva path, he should always be mindful of inhalation and exhalation. When [a bodhisattva] inhales and exhales, he counts from one to ten. In each [count] he does not let his mind be distracted. By this method, the bodhisattva attains single-mindedness and removes desirous conduct pertaining to the five obstacles.

At the Way of Seeing, a bodhisattva should practice three elements of recognition, namely the recognition of sentient beings, the recognition conforming to the Dharma, and the recognition of non-arising elements.

What is the recognition of sentient beings? If all sentient beings slander, beat, or kill [a bodhisattva], or do various evil things [to him], he is not upset, hateful, or angry. He not only endures this [treatment] but also shows friendliness and compassion to those sentient beings. He seeks various good things [for those beings] and wishes that [they] attain everything. He [thus] keeps [them] in his mind. Then [they are] gradually [made to] understand the reality of [all] elements, as if [a garment] were impregnated with a scent.

It is just like a tender mother who loves and breastfeeds her baby. She does not mind [the baby's] various filthy things but with ever-increasing love wants to help it attain pleasure. Likewise is the practitioner. [Even if] all sentient beings do various evils, his mind is not encouraged or discouraged by their pure or impure practices. He does not regress or turn back. Then [he thinks], "I will exhaustively save boundless sentient beings in the ten directions and make them attain the full awakening of the buddhas." Patiently his mind does not regress, regret, or withdraw. Nor is it indolent, weary, afraid, or worried. He single-mindedly fixes his mind on this recognition of sentient beings. He meditates on it in three ways and does not let his mind be distracted. If his mind is distracted, he concentrates it and returns it [to the original objects of meditation]. This is called the recognition of sentient beings.

What is the recognition conforming to the Dharma? The bodhisattva has already attained the recognition of sentient beings, which has boundless merits. He knows that the happy rewards of these merits are impermanent. Then he is weary of impermanence and seeks for eternal happiness. Also he seeks the everlasting Dharma for sentient beings. Whether material or immaterial, visible or invisible, tangible or intangible, defiled or undefiled, conditioned or unconditioned, superior, medium, or inferior, he seeks for their reality. What is the reality? It is not permanent or impermanent, pleasant or unpleasant, empty or non-empty, or with soul or without soul.

Why is it not permanent? It is because [the elements] arise based on causes and conditions, because what did not exist before now exist, and because they will not exist any more after having existed. For these reasons, [their reality] is not permanent.

Why is it not impermanent? It is because retribution for karma will not be lost, because [the internal elements] perceive external objects, and because the causes and conditions [of these elements] increase. For these reasons, [their reality] is not impermanent.

Why is it not pleasant? It is because a new pain is considered to be comfort,[79] because everything is by nature impermanent, and because [everything] arises conditioned by desire. For these reasons, [their reality] is not pleasant. 285b

Why is it not unpleasant? It is because there is pleasant sensation, because [elements] arise from the defilement of desire, and because one does not spare any effort to seek for pleasure. For these reasons, [their reality] is not unpleasant.

Why is it not empty? It is because each of the internal and external realms of cognition is clearly perceived, because there is retribution for sinful and meritorious [deeds], and because all sentient beings believe in [the existence of elements]. For these reasons, [their reality] is not empty.

Why is it not non-empty? It is because [elements] arise from the combination [of their causes and conditions], because one cannot perceive [the existence of elements] when one analyzes them, and because they can be transformed by the power of the mind [of a meditator]. For these reasons, they are not non-empty.

Why is it not with soul? It is because [the elements] are not independent, because the constituent element of the seventh consciousness [that could be the soul] cannot be perceived, and because the characteristics of the soul cannot be perceived. For these reasons, [their reality] is not with soul.

Why is it not without soul? It is because there are afterlives, because one attains deliverance, and because every [being] gives rise to the ego-mind and does not think of others. For these reasons, [their reality] is not without soul.

Thus, [elements] do not arise or cease. Nor is it that they do not arise or cease, existent or nonexistent. One does not experience [them] or is attached to [them]. All verbal expressions disappear and mental activities are severed; it is just like the nature of nirvana. This is the reality of [all] elements. One's faith in this Dharma is pure without stagnation or hindrances. [Thus one] easily knows, believes in, and progresses in [this Dharma]. This is called the recognition conforming to the Dharma.

What is the recognition of non-arising elements? Wisdom, faith, and diligence increase [for those of] superior capacity in the aforementioned Dharma of the reality. This is called the recognition of non-arising elements. In the Dharma of auditors, wisdom, faith, and diligence increase at the stages of heat and summit and [as a result] one attains the stage of recognition. The recognition is so called because it is the recognition of nirvana and the recognition of undefiled elements. Since one attains and sees something anew, it is called "recognition." In the case of the recognition of [non-arising] elements, the matter is the same.

Arhats whose deliverance depends on timing[80] do not attain the wisdom of non-rebirth. If they make progress and become [arhats] whose deliverance does not depend on timing, they attain the wisdom of non-rebirth. Likewise is the recognition of non-arising elements.

If those who have not attained the fruit of bodhisattvas attain the recognition of non-arising elements, they attain the true fruits of the practice of bodhisattvas. They are called the fruits of the bodhisattva path. At that time, they attain the concentration in which buddhas appear, attain great compassion for sentient beings, and enter the gate of the perfection of wisdom (*prajñāpāramitā*).

Then buddhas grant [them] the title.[81] [The bodhisattvas] are born in the realm of buddhas and are kept in mind by the buddhas. All [their] grave transgressions become light, and [their] light ones cease. The three bad destinies are severed, and [the bodhisattvas] are always born in heavens and among humankind. [Then the bodhisattvas] are called "those who do not retrogress" and reach the immovable stage. Eventually the physical body is exhausted, [and they] enter into the Dharma body, can do various supernatural performances, and save all sentient beings. [Those bodhisattvas] are endowed with the six perfections, serve buddhas, purify buddha fields, and teach sentient beings. [The bodhisattvas] are established in the ten stages, [their] merits are completed, and they gradually attain the unsurpassable awakening. This is the first gate of the methods of meditation for bodhisattvas.

> When a practitioner in concentrated mind seeks awakening, he should always observe the time and method. If he does not get the [right] time and method, that would be harmful and not beneficial. (SauN 16.49)

285c

> If one milks [a cow] when calves have not been born, milk cannot be obtained because it is not the right time. Even if calves have been born, if one milks the horn of the cow, milk cannot be obtained because of ignorance. (SauN 16.50)

> If one tries to make a fire by rubbing damp sticks together, a fire cannot be obtained because it is not the right time. If one seeks a fire by chopping a dry log, fire cannot be obtained because of ignorance. (SauN 16.51)

> One gets the place, knows the time, and measures one's own practice. One observes the method of [controlling one's own] mind, how much one's power is, what proper and improper efforts are, and when the time is proper and improper for practice. (SauN 16.52)

> If one's mind is agitated, one should not encourage [it]. Such over-encouragement is not conducive to concentration. It is just like a big fire with much wood that cannot be blown out by a heavy wind. (SauN 16.53)

> If one can control one's own mind by concentration, then the mind attains concentration by ceasing the movement [of mind]. It is just like a great fire being blown by a heavy wind, but which will be extinguished without fail when much water is poured [over it]. (SauN 16.54)

> If one's mind is languid and indolent, then the calming [method] should not be employed. It is just like a fire with little wood and without flames that will be extinguished by itself without being blown by wind. (SauN 16.55)

If one has a diligent and courageous mind, then one will become stronger and soon attain awakening. It is just like a small fire that will never be extinguished when there is more wood and a heavier wind. (SauN 16.56)

If one practices indifference to stop agitation or shrinking [of mind], even if one attains equanimity [temporarily], one will [eventually] lose it. It is just like a sick person who is must be taken care of and who, if neglected, cannot survive. (SauN 16.57)

If one is to practice the thought of indifference,[82] [when one's] mind is balanced is the right time [to do so]. [If] one [thus] practices, one will promptly attain awakening. It is just like a man riding a trained elephant who will reach a haven as he wishes without [the elephant's] stumbling. (SauN 16.58)

If lust is predominant [in a person], and if desire disturbs his mind, then he should not practice friendliness and so forth. If a lustful person practices friendliness, it will further promote unintelligent discontent. It is just like a person who suffers from excessive sensitivity to cold and takes a cooling medicine. (SauN 16.59)

A lustful person [whose] mind is disturbed should observe impurities. By observing impurities the mind can be settled, because the temperament and the practice thus correspond. It is just like a person who suffers from excessive sensitivity to cold and takes a warming medicine. (SauN 16.60)

If anger is predominant, and if resentment disturbs his mind, then he should not observe impurities. If an angry person observes disagreeable things, it will further promote the angry mind. It is just like a person who suffers from a feverish disease and takes a warming medicine. (SauN 16.61)

If a person is resentful, he should cultivate friendly mind. If he practices friendliness without interruption, the angry mind will cease, because temperament and practice thus correspond. It is just like a person who suffers from a feverish disease and takes a cooling medicine. (SauN 16.62)

If ignorance is predominant, and if the mind is dark and shallow, [one should not employ] the practice methods of impurities and friendliness, both of which would increase unintelligence and are useless. It is just like a person who suffers from a disease of wind and takes a medicine of flour. (SauN 16.63)

If a person's mind is unintelligent, he should observe dependent origination. If he analyzes and clearly observes it, the unintelligent mind will cease, because the temperament and the practice thus correspond. It is just like a person who suffers from the disease of wind and takes a greasy medicine. (SauN 16.64)

For example, [when] a goldsmith uses bellows to kindle charcoal, [if] he takes measures in an untimely [fashion, namely] hastily kindling [the fire] at the wrong time, sprinkling water [over it], or leaving [it alone at the wrong time], his use of the bellows will be unsuccessful. (SauN 16.65)

If he kindles [fire] vigorously when the gold has [already] melted, [the gold] will melt too much. If he stops [kindling the fire when the gold] has not melted, it will not melt. If he sprinkles water at the wrong time, the gold will be unfinished. If he leaves it alone at the wrong time, it will not complete [its formation]. (SauN 16.66)

One should consider the methods of practice, [namely] diligence, concentration, and indifference. Untimely methods will lose the benefit of the Dharma. If it is not to the benefit of the Dharma, it will not be beneficial. (SauN 16.67)

Just like a physician who gives medicines respectively to cure the three diseases of cold, fever, and wind, the Buddha treats the diseases of lust, anger, and ignorance by applying appropriate medicines. (SauN 16.69)

Notes

1 Also known as Māndhātā. He was a prosperous king who eventually ascended to the top of Mount Sumeru and shared a throne with Indra. However, he wanted to monopolize the throne, and due to this evil thought he fell to the ground and died. He is mentioned again later in the text (277b, p. 43).

2 I.e., to be satisfied of its desire.

3 In other words, they get weary of the impure body.

4 This would mean that his mind is easily irritable.

5 This probably means that he receives the wrong teaching from his teacher and as a result loses his sense of right and wrong.

6 I.e., the teaching of Buddhism that helps people cross the river of samsara.

7 The reference is unclear.

8 Cf. 275c, pp. 32–32, and 277c–278a, pp. 44–45, of the text.

9 At the introductory level, the first two and the last two links of the formula of dependent origination are contemplated. At the intermediate level, the third through tenth links are contemplated. At the advanced level, all twelve links are contemplated. As the practitioner becomes more experienced, he increases the items he meditates on.

10 The source is unclear.

11 Note that the primary meaning of "karma" is "action," though it also means a kind of force that is created by one's action and influences one's subsequent conditions. Here, in this context, "karma" means action itself.

12 I.e., a monk's robe.

13 This probably means that those who were the family members of the child in a past life consider those who are his/her family members in the present life to be false.

14 I.e., hell.

15 This line has no correspondent in the *Saundarananda.*

16 As we see from the following lines, here the accidents mentioned above are personified and compared to murderers.

17 In this context, these functions should refer to the "laziness, sleepiness, and heaviness in one's body" mentioned below.

18 Cf. *Treatise on the Great Perfection of Wisdom* (T25:109a).

19 The hands, feet, shoulders, and back of the neck of the Buddha are said to have had protuberances.

20 Cf. number 54 of the eighty minor bodily marks, p. 37.

21 Literally, "encounter."

22 Cf. number 23 of the thirty-two major marks, p. 35.

23 This list largely corresponds to that in the *Mohe bore boluomi jing* (Taishō no. 223; T8:395c–396b), also translated by Kumārajīva. However, this forty-ninth item has no corresponding element in the *Mohe bore boluomi jing*. The lists in the corresponding Sanskrit texts, the *Pañcaviṃśatisāhasrikā Prajñāpāramitā* and the *Aṣṭādaśa-sāhasrikā Prajñāpāramitā*, are very different from the one in the *Mohe bore boluomi jing*. Accordingly, we cannot confirm the original Sanskrit expression here.

24 The nine apertures of ordinary people leak impurities (cf. 281c, p. 65, of the text). "Filled apertures" probably implies that the body of the Buddha does not release any impurities.

25 Cf. *Treatise on the Great Perfection of Wisdom* (T25:219b–c).

26 See 276a, p. 33, of the text.

27 Also known as Māndhātā. See 270a, p. 3, and note 1 of the text.

28 I.e., a universal monarch (*cakravartin*). There are four classes of universal monarchs—gold, silver, copper, and iron—of which "king turning a golden wheel" is the highest.

29 This probably refers to the story of deer that are lured by hunters mimicking the call of a mother deer, and are then killed.

30 "Four types of donations" are the four items that are typically mentioned in early Buddhist texts, namely, food and drink, clothing, bedding, and medicine.

31 This is what the Chinese original states. However, there is no discussion of reflection and investigation in the preceding portions. Perhaps something is missing before this line.

32 Lit., "protection." We translate the underlying Sanskrit *upekṣā*.

33 A somewhat similar explanation is found in the *Śrāvakabhūmi* portion of the *Yogācārabhūmi* (Taishō no. 1579; T30:469a–470b).

34 Cf. *Treatise on the Great Perfection of Wisdom* (T25:97c).

35   A similar argument is found in the *Saṃyuktāgama* (Taishō no. 99[494]; T2:128c–129a).

36   The basic principle here is that the minds of supernatural transformation of a certain stage must be based on the same or higher stage of meditation. Lower stages of meditation cannot create the minds of transformation of advanced stages. See the *Abhidharmakośa-bhāṣya* (Taishō no. 1558; T29:144a–b).

37   Cf. *Treatise on the Great Perfection of Wisdom* (T25:105a).

38   I.e., meditation on impurities, friendliness, dependent origination, mindful breathing, and calling the Buddha to mind that are explained above.

39   Very similar arguments are found in the *Abhidharmakośa-bhāṣya* (T29:114c–115a) and the **Tattvasiddhi* (Taishō no. 1646; T32:282b).

40   "The internal mind" seems to refer to one's own mind, while "the external mind" seems to refer to the mind of someone else—though there are other interpretations of these terms as well. See the *Abhidharma-mahāvibhāṣā* (Taishō no. 1545; T27:940b).

41   Literally, "master." The underlying Sanskrit seems to be *svāmin,* which means "proprietor" or "master."

42   "The beginning of the world" is repeated in the original. One of these phrases has been omitted in this translation.

43   Meditative practice without the direct realization of the Four Noble Truths is considered to be the "defiled path," because the practitioner has not attained pure wisdom.

44   The original Sanskrit must be *pṛthagjana.*

45   See the *Dhammapada* (Taishō no. 210; T4:571b). See also a variant version of the *Saṃyuktāgama* (Taishō no. 100; T2:374c). We thank Prof. McRae for the latter reference.

46   What these verses mean seems to be something like the following: When a practitioner attains the stage of "summit" (a preliminary stage prior to awakening), he gets a reputation as an advanced practitioner. This reputation, however, could make him arrogant and bring about retrogression from that stage. According to the Sarvāstivāda tenets, until the stage of summit one could retrogress, but if one goes beyond this stage, one never retrogresses. Thus, this stage is like a mountain pass that goes over a summit.

47   "Conditioned elements not associated with the mind" is a category of elements postulated in the Sarvāstivāda system. They refer to some concepts necessary in this system, like "acquisition," "type of beings," and "life force."

48   "Acquisition" (*prāpti*) is an element that is considered to belong to the category of "conditioned elements not associated with the mind" in the Sarvāstivāda tradition. This element links a certain element to a sentient being.

49 Namely, the wisdom of origin, the wisdom of extinction, and the wisdom of the path.

50 Cf. *Abhidharma-prakaraṇa* (Taishō no. 1541; T26:628b).

51 As will be stated below, there are altogether nine classes of binding defilements belonging to the realm of desire. In principle, defilements are severed by undefiled wisdom, which is attained only after entering the Way of Seeing (*darśana-mārga*). According to the Sarvāstivāda tenets, however, one can also sever defilements by worldly meditation (which is called the "defiled path") even before entering the Way of Seeing.

52 Literally, "common people." Cf. 279c, p. 54, of the text, where the interlineal note criticizes this translation and supports another translation, "wild person." In the Sarvāstivāda system, "unawakened people" refer to those who have not entered the Way of Seeing.

53 In order to be reborn in the realm of desire, one must have defilements belonging to the realm of desire. If one has severed the nine classes of (i.e., all) defilements belonging to the realm of desire, one will never be reborn in (in other words, return to) the realm of desire. Thus, one is called "non-returner" (*anāgāmin*).

54 According to Sarvāstivāda tenets, it takes two steps to sever any class of defilement: "the immediate path" and "the path of deliverance." What the text refers to here is the very last moment of severing the defilements belonging to the realm of desire.

55 Cf. **Miśrakābhidharmahṛdaya* (Taishō no. 1552; T28: 913c).

56 Once one enters the Way of Seeing, one cannot be reborn for the eighth time.

57 "The three vows" should refer to those described just above.

58 Namely, the realms of animals, hungry ghosts, and hells.

59 Literally, free from dye.

60 *Mahāsattva*s, i.e., bodhisattvas.

61 This story appears in the *Ratnakūṭa* collection (Taishō no. 310(291); T11: 543a–b); pointed out in *Kokuyaku issaikyō: Kyōshū bu* 4:321, n. 167.

62 Namely, pleasant, painful, and neutral ones. See below.

63 From the fourth stage of meditation upward, there is only neutral sensation. See 278a, p. 46, of the text.

64 Namely, the first three of the four stages of meditation.

65 Namely, from the realm of boundless space to the realm neither with nor without ideation. See below.

66 The five aggregates (*skandha*s) are classified into one material aggregate (form) and four immaterial aggregates (sensation, ideation, conduct, and consciousness, i.e., "name").

67 "Name" and form (*nāma-rūpa*) is a fixed compound referring to one's total existence consisting of mental ("name") and physical (form) elements. This line is a gloss of that compound.

68 In the Buddhist system, any perception requires three elements: a sense organ, a cognitive object, and consciousness. Here, the eye is the sense organ, a piece of matter is a cognitive object, and the visual consciousness is consciousness.

69 "The heaven where one can enjoy the supernatural creations of other deities" is the highest heaven in the realm of desire.

70 To call karma "existence" might sound a little strange, but in the Sarvāstivāda system "existence" (*bhava*) is usually interpreted as the karma that brings about the subsequent link, "birth."

71 Sense organ, cognitive object, and consciousness. See note 68.

72 There might be some textual confusion here. Perhaps the intended reading is something like: "The sprout is not identical with or separate from the seed."

73 Literally, "existence."

74 Perhaps this should be corrected to "no characteristics," as in 283c12, p. 75, of the text.

75 A few characters seem to be missing here.

76 These are collectively called the "eightfold straight path."

77 Probably in this context this refers to unconditioned elements (*asaṃskṛta*).

78 Cf. *Treatise on the Middle* (T30:2b–3c).

79 Cf. 278c, p. 49, of the text.

80 This refers to those who enter concentration only when favorable conditions for practice are provided. See the *Abhidharmakośa-bhāṣya* (T29:129a–b).

81 This seems to mean that the practitioners are formally recognized as bodhisattvas.

82 Literally, "one has a thought of indifference," which is a little unclear. This is a free translation based on the context. We also referred to the Sanskrit text of the *Saundarananda*.

Glossary

anāgāmin (non-returner): The third of the four stages of spiritual attainment in the vehicle of auditors; one who has attained this stage is no longer subject to rebirth in the realm of desire. *See also* vehicle; three realms.

arhat: A practitioner who has completely eradicated the defilements and attained liberation from the cycle of birth and death (samsara); the highest of the four stages of spiritual attainment in the vehicle of auditors. *See also* vehicle; samsara.

auditor (*śrāvaka*): Originally, a disciple of the Buddha, one of those who heard him expound the teachings directly; later, the term came to refer to practitioners aiming at becoming arhats rather than buddhas. *See also* arhat; vehicle.

awakening (*bodhi*): The attainment of wisdom free from defilement. This wisdom liberates one from samsara and leads one to nirvana. *See also* nirvana; samsara.

bad destiny: Refers to rebirth in one of the three lower worlds of samsaric existence, the worlds of of animals, hungry ghosts (*pretas*), or hell. *See also* samsara.

bodhisattva: One who has made a resolve to attain the highest awakening of buddhas on behalf of all sentient beings; practitioners of Mahayana. In the course of their spiritual careers, bodhisattvas engage in the practice of the six perfections (*pāramitās*) and attain stages of increasingly higher levels of spiritual accomplishment. See also Mahayana; six perfections.

bodhi tree: The tree under which a buddha attains enlightenment.

buddhahood: The state of becoming or being a buddha; the goal of the bodhisattva path.

calming and contemplation (*śamatha* and *vipaśyanā*): The two phases of meditation; the first phase, consisting of calming the mind and stilling discursive thoughts, prepares a stable base for the second phase, meditative insight into reality.

concentration (*samādhi*): A state in which the mind is concentrated on one point.

dependent origination (*pratītyasamutpāda*): The Buddhist doctrine that explains the causal chain of samsaric existence, which usually consists of twelve links, beginning with ignorance and ending in old age and death.

Dharma: The truth, law; the teachings of the Buddha.

Dharma body (*dharmakāya*): Ultimate reality as the essence of a buddha.

eightfold correct path: Correct view, correct thought, correct speech, correct action, correct livelihood, correct effort, correct mindfulness, and correct meditation. Also translated in this text as the eightfold straight path. This constitutes the fourth of the Four Noble Truths, the path leading to nirvana, or liberation from samsara. *See also* Four Noble Truths; nirvana; samsara.

emptiness (*śūnyatā*): The absence of substantiality of the self and all phenomena (*dharma*s), which arise only contingent on causes and conditions.

five aggregates (*skandha*s): The five elements of form, sensation, ideation, conduct, and consciousness that comprise the personality and are misconceived by deluded beings as a substantial self.

four continents: In Buddhist cosmology, the four large land masses in one of the oceans around Mount Sumeru. Each continent is in one of the cardinal directions, and human beings live on these continents. *See also* Mount Sumeru.

four gross elements: The four physical elements that constitute material phenomena, namely, earth, water, fire, and wind.

Four Noble Truths: The basic doctrine of Buddhism: 1) the truth of suffering, 2) the truth of the origin of suffering, 3) the truth of the extinction of suffering, and 4) the truth of the path that leads to the extinction of suffering, i.e., nirvana. *See also* nirvana.

karma: Lit., "action." Any mental, verbal, or physical act that leads to rebirth in samsara. Morally good, evil, and neutral karma brings about, respectively, comfortable, uncomfortable, and neutral fruit. *See also* samsara.

Mahayana: ("Great Vehicle"): A form of Buddhism that developed in India around the beginning of the common era, practitioners of which are considered to be bodhisattvas, magnanimous beings who aspire to the highest awakening (*bodhicitta*) on behalf of all sentient beings. *See also* bodhisattva.

mindfulness: A fundamental Buddhist practice of maintaining awareness and clear observation in meditation and during all one's activities, physical or mental, in order to bring the mind under control and to a state of rest and provide a stable basis for wisdom and insight.

Mount Sumeru: In Buddhist cosmology, the highest mountain rising from the center of the world, surrounded by oceans in which the four continents that comprise the world of human beings are situated. *See also* four continents.

nirvana: Liberation from samsara, a state in which all passions are extinguished. One is led to this state through awakening. *See also* awakening; samsara.

prajñā: The wisdom to comprehend the Buddhist truth; one of the six perfections. *See also* six perfections.

sakṛdāgāmin (once-returner): The second of the four stages of spiritual attainment in the vehicle of auditors; one who has attained this state is subject to rebirth once in the realm of desire and once in the upper realms before attaining nirvana. *See also* nirvana; three realms; vehicle.

Śākyamuni: The historical Buddha, who lived in India in the fifth century B.C.E. and whose life and teachings form the basis for Buddhism.

samsara: The cycle of existence, the continuous cycle of birth and death through which beings transmigrate; the world of suffering, contrasted with the liberation of nirvana. *See also* nirvana.

Śāriputra: A principal disciple of the Buddha.

Sarvāstivāda: A school of Traditional Buddhism that holds that all phenomena, including past and future, exist substantially.

sense faculties: The six sense organs, namely, the eyes, ears, nose, tongue, body, and mind, which in contact with their corresponding sense objects result in visual, auditory, olfactory, gustatory, tactile, and mental perceptions.

six perfections (*pāramitā*s): Six qualities to be perfected by bodhisattvas on their way to complete awakening: 1) alms or giving (*dāna*), 2) discipline or morality (*śīla*), 3) forbearance or patience (*kṣānti*), 4) exertion or diligence (*vīrya*), 5) meditation (*dhyāna*), and 6) wisdom (*prajñā*). See also bodhisattva.

skillful means (*upāya*): The various methods and means used by buddhas, bodhisattvas, and other Buddhist practitioners.

solitary awakened one (*pratyekabuddha*): According to common understanding, a solitary awakened one attains liberation through direct observation and understanding of the principle of dependent origination without the guidance of a teacher, and does not teach others. See also auditor; dependent orgination.

srotāpanna (stream-entrant): The first of the four stages of spiritual attainment in the vehicle of auditors; one who has entered the stream of the Dharma by destroying various wrong views at the Way of Seeing. See also vehicle; Way of Seeing.

Three Jewels: Buddha, Dharma (the teachings), and Sangha (the monastic community).

three poisons: The three cardinal defilements, namely lust (or greed), anger (or hatred), and ignorance (or delusion).

three realms: the realm of desire (*kāmadhātu*), i.e., the world of ordinary consciousness accompanied by desires; the realm of form (*rūpadhātu*), in which desires have been eliminated but material phenomena remain; and the realm without form (*ārūpya-dhātu*), in which material phenomena no longer exist. See also samsara.

Traditional Buddhism: A term for various early schools of Buddhism that deem only traditional scriptures (*āgamas/nikāyas*) authoritative and do not accept the authority of Mahayana scriptures. Often referred to as "Hinayana" ("Small Vehicle") by Mahayanists. *See also* Mahayana.

vehicle (*yāna*): The various Buddhist paths of practice, of which typically three are enumerated, namely the vehicle of auditors (*śrāvaka*s), culminating in arhatship; the vehicle of solitary awakened ones (*pratyekabuddha*s); and the vehicle of bodhisattvas, culminating in buddhahood. *See also* auditor; bodhisattva; Mahayana; solitary awakened one.

Vinaya: Precepts and rules of conduct for monastics.

Way of Seeing (*darśana-mārga*): The stage of practice at which practitioners directly perceive the Buddhist truth and free themselves from wrong views.

wheel-turning king (*cakravartin*): The ideal king, as conceived of in India; also called universal ruler.

Yogācāra: A school of Buddhist thought systematized by the Indian masters Asaṅga and Vasubandhu in the fourth century C.E., focused on meditative practice and a detailed analysis of mind.

Bibliography

Demiéville, Paul. "La *Yogācārabhūmi* de Saṅgharakṣa" ("The *Yogācārabhūmi* of Saṅgharakṣa"). *Bulletin de l'École Française d'Extrême-Orient* 44/2 (1854): 339–436.

Lamotte, Étienne. *Le traité de la grande vertu de sagesse de Nāgārjuna* (*The Treatise on the Great Virtue of Wisdom of Nāgārjuna*). 5 vols. Louvain-La-Neuve: Insitut Orientaliste, Université de Louvain, 1970–1981.

Matsunami, Seiren. *Memyō Tansei naru Nanda* (*Aśvaghoṣa, Saundarananda*). Tokyo: Sankibō Busshorin, 1981.

Satō, Taishun, trans. *Kokuyaku issaikyō kyōshūbu* (*Japanese Translation of Chinese Buddhist Canon: Miscellaneous Sutras*), vol. 4. Tokyo: Daitō Shuppansha, 1931.

Xinjiang Qiuci Shiku Yanjiusuo (Kucha Caves Research Institute of Xinjiang), ed. *Jiumo luoshi he Zhongguo minzu wenhua* (*Kumārajīva and Chinese National Culture*). Urumqi: Xinjiang Meishu Sheying Chubanshe, 2001.

Tran Thuy Khanh. "*Zazen sanmai kyō* ni okeru bosatsu no go kanpō to *Dai chido ron* tono kanren ni tsuite" ("The Relationship between the Five Views of the Bodhisattva in the *Zuochan sanmai jing* and the *Mahāprajñāpāramitā-śāstra*"). *Indogaku bukkyōgaku kenkyū* (*Journal of Indian and Buddhist Studies*) 56/2 (2008): 967–971.

Yamabe, Nobuyoshi. "The Paths of Śrāvakas and Bodhisattvas in Meditative Practices." *Acta Asiatica* 96 (2009): 47–75.

Index

A

Abhidharmakośa-bhāṣya 91, 93
Abhidharma-mahāvibhāṣā xvii, 91
Abhidharma-prakaraṇa 92
abode 5, 7, 27, 46, 50
ache 71–72, 79
Acts of the Buddha xvii
agony(ies) (*see also* suffering) 22, 23,
    25, 34, 47, 49, 53
Akaniṣṭha Heaven 59, 73
Amoghavajra xiv
anāgāmin(s) xvi, 57, 58, 59, 92
anger (*see also* three poisons) xiv, 7, 10,
    14, 15, 16, 19, 20, 21, 22, 47, 49, 66,
    69, 73, 86, 87
    method of curing 14–16, 66–70
An Shigeo xviii
anuttarā samyaksaṃbodhi. See awaken-
    ing, full, great, unsurpassable
arhat(s) xiv, xv, xvi, 20, 22, 24, 26, 54,
    59, 60, 61, 66, 70, 80, 84
    nine types of 59
ārūpyadhātu. See realm, formless, with-
    out form
Aśoka, King xvii
Aṣṭādaśasāhasrikā Prajñāpāramitā 90
asura. See demon
Aśvaghoṣa xv, xvi, xvii
attachment(s) (*see also* dependent origi-
    nation, twelve links of) 4, 6, 11, 12,
    16, 17, 20, 23, 24, 53, 66
    to relatives 23, 24
    seven types of 11

auditor(s) 62, 84
Avīci Hell 73
avidyā. See ignorance
awakening 6, 19, 20, 21, 22, 26, 27, 38,
    39, 43, 56, 58, 61, 67, 85, 86, 91
    full, great, unsurpassable xv, 39, 61,
    62, 63, 64, 68, 82, 85
    seven elements of 27, 79, 80

B

banyan tree 35
being(s) (*see also* human being; sentient
    being) 22, 23, 25, 63, 66, 69, 81, 82,
    83, 91
bhava. See existence
bimba fruit 36
binding defilements, bond(s), bondage
    5, 17, 19, 25, 27, 32, 33, 44, 55, 56,
    57–59, 64, 75, 92
birth (*see also* dependent origination,
    twelve links of; rebirth) 16, 17, 20,
    26, 54, 69, 70, 73, 74, 75, 81, 93
Blessed One(s) 48, 54, 70
bodhisattva(s) 54, 63, 64, 65, 67, 70, 74,
    75, 79, 81, 82, 84–85, 92, 93
    path xv, 64, 66, 70, 82, 84
bodhi tree 38, 40
body(ies) xiv, 3, 5, 8, 10, 11, 12, 13, 14,
    15, 19, 21, 23, 24, 25, 28, 31, 43, 47,
    48, 49, 51, 52, 53, 59, 62, 64, 65, 66,
    67, 69, 71, 73, 74, 79, 84, 89, 90
    of buddhas, Buddha 35, 36, 37, 38,
    39, 62, 63, 64, 90

meditation(s) (*continued*)
  on calling the Buddha to mind 27
  on dependent origination 10
  on extinction 60
  first stage 13, 31, 43, 44, 45, 48
  five obstacles of 30, 82
  four stages of xv, xvi, 27, 48, 60, 92
  fourth stage 46, 47, 48, 72, 92
  heatless 44
  on ignorance 18
  on impermanence 75
  on the impurities xiv, xvi, xvii, 10–11, 27, 64–65, 91
  Mahayanist xiv, xv, xviii
  manual(s) xiii, xiv, xvii, xviii
  method(s) xiv, xviii, 27, 48, 85
  object(s) of 5, 12, 13, 14, 16, 17, 27, 38, 64, 65, 66, 74, 82
  pure, on the pure 13, 14
  on the reality of all elements 12
  second stage 31, 45, 47, 48
  third stage 32, 45, 46, 47, 48
  three classes of 12
  Traditional xiv, xv
  Way of 79
mental 32, 34, 44, 50, 56, 72, 75
  actions, activity(ies) 27, 45, 84
  agonies, suffering 22, 25, 34
  conduct 71–72
  defilements 52, 57
  element(s) 33, 45, 67, 72, 93
  eye 15, 33, 34, 63, 66
  functions 31, 56, 80
  image, imagination 33, 34, 38
merit(s) 7, 26, 44, 46, 51, 55, 60, 61, 63, 64, 65, 66, 69, 71, 79, 82, 85
  enemies, thieves of 22, 43
  roots of 21, 22, 53–54, 55, 57–58, 59, 61
meritorious 3, 39, 58, 63
  acts, deeds 8, 10, 69, 83

method(s) xv, xviii, xxi, 6, 7, 12, 30, 33, 45, 46, 79, 82, 85, 87
  five xiv–xv, xxi, 10, 48
  meditation xiv, xviii, xxi, 27, 48, 85
  calming 85
  of calling the Buddha to mind 10
  of concentration on friendliness 10, 16, 67–69, 87
  of contemplation 29–30
  of counting, following the breath, mindful breathing 10, 18, 27–29
  of curing anger 14–16
  of curing discursive thoughts 18–33
  of curing ignorance 16–18
  of curing lust 10–14
  of curing people equally troubled with multiple problems 33–41
  of fixing the mind 29
  of impurities 10, 87
  of meditation on dependent origination 10
  six 18, 27
  sixteen 30–33
mind(s) (*see also* calling the Buddha to mind) 3, 4, 5, 6, 7, 8, 9, 10, 12, 13, 14–15, 16, 17, 18, 19, 20, 21, 22, 23, 24, 25, 27, 28, 29, 30, 31, 32, 33, 34, 39, 40, 41, 43, 44, 45, 47, 49, 50–51, 52, 53, 54, 55, 56, 60, 62–63, 64, 65, 66, 67, 68, 69, 72, 73, 74, 78, 79, 80, 83, 84, 85, 86, 87, 89, 91
  compassionate 47, 75
  concentrated, fixed, undistracted 13, 29, 32, 45, 48, 53, 74, 85
  desirous, envious, lustful 22, 44, 50
  distracted 12, 13, 14, 16, 17, 32, 34, 38, 40, 63, 64, 65, 66, 74. 82
  equanimous, tranquil 13, 45, 47
  evil, perverted, wicked 5, 12, 32, 36
  external 51, 91
  four balanced 60

of space 46, 73, 92

three 24

rebirth (*see also* birth) 7, 8, 39, 41, 43, 73, 84

recognition xvi, 30, 55, 56–57, 81, 82, 84

stage of 30, 55, 84

reflection 46, 67, 78

and investigation 45, 71, 90

retrogress, retrogression 40, 59–60, 61, 84, 91

rūpadhātu. See realm, of form

S

Saddharmapuṇḍarīka-sūtra. See Lotus Sutra

ṣaḍāyatana. See cognition, six realms of

sakṛdāgāmin(s) xvi, 57, 58, 59, 61

sage(s) 4, 39, 43, 45, 53

Śākyamuni (*see also* Buddha) 34

śamatha 51–52

samsara 5, 6, 23, 26, 34, 39, 64, 65, 68, 89

saṃskāra. See conduct

Saṃyuktāgama 91

Saṅgharakṣa xv, xvi, xvii

Yogācārabhūmi of xvii

Saṅghasena xv, xvi, xvii

Sanskrit xxi, 54, 90, 91, 93

Śāriputra 60, 61

Sarvāstivāda xvii, 91, 92, 93

Saundarananda xvii, xviii, xxi, 89, 93

scripture(s) (*see also* sutra) xiv, 75

self 17, 45, 48, 74, 75, 76

without (*see also* no-self) xv, 32, 48, 49, 52, 55, 75

Sengrui xiv, xv, xvi, xvii, xviii

sensation(s) (*see also* dependent origination, twelve links of) 16, 17, 50, 51, 70, 72–73, 92

comfortable, pleasant 31, 49, 50, 72, 73, 83

mindfulness to xv, 30, 31, 50

neutral 50, 72, 73, 92

painful 50, 72, 73

sense(s), sense faculties 4, 12

sense object(s) (see also object, cognitive, sense) 40, 52, 74

sense organs 73, 74, 93

sentient being(s) (*see also* beings; human beings) 3, 5, 15, 17, 21, 22, 24, 25, 26, 27, 36, 37, 38, 39, 41, 44, 47, 48, 60, 63, 64, 65, 66, 67, 68, 70, 73, 75, 77, 79, 81, 82, 83, 84, 85, 91

single-minded, single-mindedly, single-mindedness xv, 4, 5, 18, 29, 30, 33, 43, 44, 45, 46, 47, 53, 54, 55, 65, 66, 67, 68, 70, 78, 79, 82

six perfections xvii, 85

skillful means 43, 45

snake(s) 16, 19, 20, 25

solitary awakened one(s) 54, 61, 62, 70

path xiv, xvii

three levels of 61

sparśa. See contact

śrāvaka. See auditor

srotāpanna xvi, 57, 58, 61

stage(s) 11, 26, 30, 45, 46, 54, 60, 79, 91

advanced xv, 46, 55, 91

attained 59, 60

first, of meditation 13, 31, 43, 44, 45, 46, 48

four, of formless concentration xv, xvi

four, of meditation xv, xvi, 48, 60, 92

four supramundane xv

fourth, of meditation 46, 47, 48, 72, 92

of heat 30, 53, 84

immovable 84

intermediate 55, 60

lower 55, 72, 91

of recognition 30, 55, 84

second, of meditation 31, 45, 47, 48

six, of mindful breathing xvi, 54

of summit 30, 54, 84, 91

BDK English Tripiṭaka
(First Series)

Abbreviations

Ch.:   Chinese
Skt.:   Sanskrit
Jp.:   Japanese
Eng.:   Published title

Title	Taishō No.
Ch. Changahanjing (長阿含經) Skt. Dīrghāgama	1
Ch. Zhongahanjing (中阿含經) Skt. Madhyamāgama	26
Ch. Dachengbenshengxindiguanjing (大乘本生心地觀經)	159
Ch. Fosuoxingzan (佛所行讚) Skt. Buddhacarita	192
Ch. Zabaocangjing (雜寶藏經) Eng. *The Storehouse of Sundry Valuables* (1994)	203
Ch. Fajupiyujing (法句譬喻經) Eng. *The Scriptural Text: Verses of the Doctrine, with Parables* (1999)	211
Ch. Xiaopinbanruoboluomijing (小品般若波羅蜜經) Skt. Aṣṭasāhasrikā-prajñāpāramitā-sūtra	227
Ch. Jingangbanruoboluomijing (金剛般若波羅蜜經) Skt. Vajracchedikā-prajñāpāramitā-sūtra	235
Ch. Daluojingangbukongzhenshisanmoyejing (大樂金剛不空眞實三麼耶經) Skt. Adhyardhaśatikā-prajñāpāramitā-sūtra	243
Ch. Renwangbanruoboluomijing (仁王般若波羅蜜經) Skt. Kāruṇikārājā-prajñāpāramitā-sūtra (?)	245

113

Title	Taishō No.
Ch. Banruoboluomiduoxingjing (般若波羅蜜多心經) Skt. Prajñāpāramitāhṛdaya-sūtra	251
Ch. Miaofalianhuajing (妙法蓮華經) Skt. Saddharmapuṇḍarīka-sūtra Eng. *The Lotus Sutra* (Revised Second Edition, 2007)	262
Ch. Wuliangyijing (無量義經)	276
Ch. Guanpuxianpusaxingfajing (觀普賢菩薩行法經)	277
Ch. Dafangguangfohuayanjing (大方廣佛華嚴經) Skt. Avataṃsaka-sūtra	278
Ch. Shengmanshizihouyichengdafangbianfangguangjing (勝鬘師子吼一乘大方便方廣經) Skt. Śrīmālādevīsiṃhanāda-sūtra Eng. *The Sutra of Queen Śrīmālā of the Lion's Roar* (2004)	353
Ch. Wuliangshoujing (無量壽經) Skt. Sukhāvatīvyūha Eng. *The Larger Sutra on Amitāyus* (in *The Three Pure Land Sutras,* Revised Second Edition, 2003)	360
Ch. Guanwuliangshoufojing (觀無量壽佛經) Skt. Amitāyurdhyāna-sūtra Eng. *The Sutra on Contemplation of Amitāyus* (in *The Three Pure Land Sutras,* Revised Second Edition, 2003)	365
Ch. Amituojing (阿彌陀經) Skt. Sukhāvatīvyūha Eng. *The Smaller Sutra on Amitāyus* (in *The Three Pure Land Sutras,* Revised Second Edition, 2003)	366
Ch. Dabanniepanjing (大般涅槃經) Skt. Mahāparinirvāṇa-sūtra	374
Ch. Fochuiboniepanlüeshuojiaojiejing (佛垂般涅槃略説教誡經) Eng. *The Bequeathed Teaching Sutra* (in *Apocryphal Scriptures,* 2005)	389
Ch. Dicangpusabenyuanjing (地藏菩薩本願經) Skt. Kṣitigarbhapraṇidhāna-sūtra (?)	412
Ch. Banzhousanmeijing (般舟三昧經) Skt. Pratyutpannabuddhasammukhāvasthitasamādhi-sūtra Eng. *The Pratyutpanna Samādhi Sutra* (1998)	418

Title	Taishō No.
Ch. Dafangguangyuanjuexiuduoluoliaoyijing (大方廣圓覺修多羅了義經)	842
Eng. *The Sutra of Perfect Enlightenment* (in *Apocryphal Scriptures,* 2005)	
Ch. Dabiluzhenachengfoshenbianjiachijing (大毘盧遮那成佛神變加持經)	848
Skt. Mahāvairocanābhisambodhivikurvitādhiṣṭhānavaipulyasūtrendra-rājanāmadharmaparyāya	
Eng. *The Vairocanābhisaṃbodhi Sutra* (2005)	
Ch. Jinggangdingyiqierulaizhenshishedachengxianzhengdajiao-wangjing (金剛頂一切如來眞實攝大乘現證大教王經)	865
Skt. Sarvatathāgatatattvasaṃgrahamahāyānābhisamayamahākalparāja	
Eng. *The Adamantine Pinnacle Sutra* (in *Two Esoteric Sutras,* 2001)	
Ch. Suxidijieluojing (蘇悉地羯囉經)	893
Skt. Susiddhikaramahātantrasādhanopāyika-paṭala	
Eng. *The Susiddhikara Sutra* (in *Two Esoteric Sutras,* 2001)	
Ch. Modengqiejing (摩登伽經)	1300
Skt. Mātaṅgī-sūtra (?)	
Ch. Mohesengqilü (摩訶僧祇律)	1425
Skt. Mahāsāṃghika-vinaya (?)	
Ch. Sifenlü (四分律)	1428
Skt. Dharmaguptaka-vinaya (?)	
Ch. Shanjianlüpiposha (善見律毘婆沙)	1462
Pāli Samantapāsādikā	
Ch. Fanwangjing (梵網經)	1484
Skt. Brahmajāla-sūtra (?)	
Ch. Youposaijiejing (優婆塞戒經)	1488
Skt. Upāsakaśīla-sūtra (?)	
Eng. *The Sutra on Upāsaka Precepts* (1994)	
Ch. Miaofalianhuajingyoubotishe (妙法蓮華經憂波提舍)	1519
Skt. Saddharmapuṇḍarīka-upadeśa	
Ch. Shih-chu-pi-p'o-sha-lun (十住毘婆沙論)	1521
Skt. Daśabhūmika-vibhāṣā (?)	
Ch. Fodijinglun (佛地經論)	1530
Skt. Buddhabhūmisūtra-śāstra (?)	
Eng. *The Interpretation of the Buddha Land* (2002)	

Title	Taishō No.
Ch. Apidamojushelun (阿毘達磨俱舍論) Skt. Abhidharmakośa-bhāṣya	1558
Ch. Zhonglun (中論) Skt. Madhyamaka-śāstra	1564
Ch. Yüqieshidilun (瑜伽師地論) Skt. Yogācārabhūmi	1579
Ch. Chengweishilun (成唯識論) Eng. *Demonstration of Consciousness Only* (in *Three Texts on Consciousness Only,* 1999)	1585
Ch. Weishisanshilunsong (唯識三十論頌) Skt. Triṃśikā Eng. *The Thirty Verses on Consciousness Only* (in *Three Texts on Consciousness Only,* 1999)	1586
Ch. Weishihershilun (唯識二十論) Skt. Viṃśatikā Eng. *The Treatise in Twenty Verses on Consciousness Only* (in *Three Texts on Consciousness Only,* 1999)	1590
Ch. Shedachenglun (攝大乘論) Skt. Mahāyānasaṃgraha Eng. *The Summary of the Great Vehicle* (Revised Second Edition, 2003)	1593
Ch. Bianzhongbianlun (辯中邊論) Skt. Madhyāntavibhāga	1600
Ch. Dachengzhuangyanjinglun (大乘莊嚴經論) Skt. Mahāyānasūtrālaṃkāra	1604
Ch. Dachengchengyelun (大乘成業論) Skt. Karmasiddhiprakaraṇa	1609
Ch. Jiujingyichengbaoxinglun (究竟一乘寶性論) Skt. Ratnagotravibhāgamahāyānottaratantra-śāstra	1611
Ch. Yinmingruzhenglilun (因明入正理論) Skt. Nyāyapraveśa	1630
Ch. Dachengjipusaxuelun (大乘集菩薩學論) Skt. Śikṣāsamuccaya	1636

Title	Taishō No.
Ch. Jingangzhenlun (金剛針論) Skt. Vajrasūcī	1642
Ch. Zhangsuozhilun (彰所知論) Eng. *The Treatise on the Elucidation of the Knowable* (2004)	1645
Ch. Putixingjing (菩提行經) Skt. Bodhicaryāvatāra	1662
Ch. Jingangdingyuqiezhongfaanouduoluosanmiaosanputixinlun (金剛頂瑜伽中發阿耨多羅三藐三菩提心論)	1665
Ch. Dachengqixinlun (大乘起信論) Skt. Mahāyānaśraddhotpāda-śāstra (?) Eng. *The Awakening of Faith* (2005)	1666
Ch. Shimoheyanlun (釋摩訶衍論)	1668
Ch. Naxianbiqiujing (那先比丘經) Pāli Milindapañhā	1670
Ch. Banruoboluomiduoxinjingyuzan (般若波羅蜜多心經幽賛) Eng. *A Comprehensive Commentary on the Heart Sutra* (*Prajñāpāramitā-hṛdaya-sūtra*) (2001)	1710
Ch. Miaofalianhuajingxuanyi (妙法蓮華經玄義)	1716
Ch. Guanwuliangshoufojingshu (觀無量壽佛經疏)	1753
Ch. Sanlunxuanyi (三論玄義)	1852
Ch. Dachengxuanlun (大乘玄論)	1853
Ch. Zhaolun (肇論)	1858
Ch. Huayanyichengjiaoyifenqizhang (華嚴一乘教義分齊章)	1866
Ch. Yuanrenlun (原人論)	1886
Ch. Mohezhiguan (摩訶止觀)	1911
Ch. Xiuxizhiguanzuochanfayao (修習止觀坐禪法要)	1915
Ch. Tiantaisijiaoyi (天台四教儀)	1931
Ch. Guoqingbailu (國清百錄)	1934
Ch. Zhenzhoulinjihuizhaochanshiwulu (鎮州臨濟慧照禪師語錄) Eng. *The Recorded Sayings of Linji* (in *Three Chan Classics*, 1999)	1985

Title	Taishō No.
Ch. Foguoyuanwuchanshibiyanlu (佛果圜悟禪師碧巖録)	2003
Eng. *The Blue Cliff Record* (1998)	
Ch. Wumenguan (無門關)	2005
Eng. *Wumen's Gate* (in *Three Chan Classics*, 1999)	
Ch. Liuzudashifabaotanjing (六祖大師法寶壇經)	2008
Eng. *The Platform Sutra of the Sixth Patriarch* (2000)	
Ch. Xinxinming (信心銘)	2010
Eng. *The Faith-Mind Maxim* (in *Three Chan Classics*, 1999)	
Ch. Huangboshanduanjichanshichuanxinfayao (黄檗山斷際禪師傳心法要)	2012A
Eng. *Essentials of the Transmission of Mind* (in *Zen Texts*, 2005)	
Ch. Yongjiazhengdaoge (永嘉證道歌)	2014
Ch. Chixiubaizhangqinggui (勅修百丈清規)	2025
Eng. *The Baizhang Zen Monastic Regulations* (2007)	
Ch. Yibuzonglunlun (異部宗輪論)	2031
Skt. Samayabhedoparacanacakra	
Eng. *The Cycle of the Formation of the Schismatic Doctrines* (2004)	
Ch. Ayuwangjing (阿育王經)	2043
Skt. Aśokāvadāna	
Eng. *The Biographical Scripture of King Aśoka* (1993)	
Ch. Mamingpusachuan (馬鳴菩薩傳)	2046
Eng. *The Life of Aśvaghoṣa Bodhisattva* (in *Lives of Great Monks and Nuns*, 2002)	
Ch. Longshupusachuan (龍樹菩薩傳)	2047
Eng. *The Life of Nāgārjuna Bodhisattva* (in *Lives of Great Monks and Nuns*, 2002)	
Ch. Posoupandoufashichuan (婆藪槃豆法師傳)	2049
Eng. *Biography of Dharma Master Vasubandhu* (in *Lives of Great Monks and Nuns*, 2002)	
Ch. Datangdaciensisancangfashichuan (大唐大慈恩寺三藏法師傳)	2053
Eng. *A Biography of the Tripiṭaka Master of the Great Ci'en Monastery of the Great Tang Dynasty* (1995)	
Ch. Gaosengchuan (高僧傳)	2059

Title	Taishō No.
Ch. Biqiunichuan (比丘尼傳) Eng. *Biographies of Buddhist Nuns* (in *Lives of Great Monks and Nuns,* 2002)	2063
Ch. Gaosengfaxianchuan (高僧法顯傳) Eng. *The Journey of the Eminent Monk Faxian* (in *Lives of Great Monks and Nuns,* 2002)	2085
Ch. Datangxiyuji (大唐西域記) Eng. *The Great Tang Dynasty Record of the Western Regions* (1996)	2087
Ch. Youfangjichao: Tangdaheshangdongzhengchuan (遊方記抄: 唐大和上東征傳)	2089-(7)
Ch. Hongmingji (弘明集)	2102
Ch. Fayuanzhulin (法苑珠林)	2122
Ch. Nanhaijiguineifachuan (南海寄歸內法傳) Eng. *Buddhist Monastic Traditions of Southern Asia* (2000)	2125
Ch. Fanyuzaming (梵語雑名)	2135
Jp. Shōmangyōgisho (勝鬘經義疏)	2185
Jp. Yuimakyōgisho (維摩經義疏)	2186
Jp. Hokkegisho (法華義疏)	2187
Jp. Hannyashingyōhiken (般若心經秘鍵)	2203
Jp. Daijōhossōkenjinshō (大乘法相研神章)	2309
Jp. Kan-jin-kaku-mu-shō (觀心覺夢鈔)	2312
Jp. Risshūkōyō (律宗綱要) Eng. *The Essentials of the Vinaya Tradition* (1995)	2348
Jp. Tendaihokkeshūgishū (天台法華宗義集) Eng. *The Collected Teachings of the Tendai Lotus School* (1995)	2366
Jp. Kenkairon (顯戒論)	2376
Jp. Sangegakushōshiki (山家學生式)	2377
Jp. Hizōhōyaku (秘藏寶鑰) Eng. *The Precious Key to the Secret Treasury* (in *Shingon Texts,* 2004)	2426

Title	Taishō No.
Jp. Benkenmitsunikyōron (辨顯密二教論)	2427
Eng. *On the Differences between the Exoteric and Esoteric Teachings* (in *Shingon Texts*, 2004)	
Jp. Sokushinjōbutsugi (即身成佛義)	2428
Eng. *The Meaning of Becoming a Buddha in This Very Body* (in *Shingon Texts*, 2004)	
Jp. Shōjijissōgi (聲字實相義)	2429
Eng. *The Meanings of Sound, Sign, and Reality* (in *Shingon Texts*, 2004)	
Jp. Unjigi (吽字義)	2430
Eng. *The Meanings of the Word Hūṃ* (in *Shingon Texts*, 2004)	
Jp. Gorinkujimyōhimitsushaku (五輪九字明秘密釋)	2514
Eng. *The Illuminating Secret Commentary on the Five Cakras and the Nine Syllables* (in *Shingon Texts*, 2004)	
Jp. Mitsugoninhotsurosangemon (密嚴院發露懺悔文)	2527
Eng. *The Mitsugonin Confession* (in *Shingon Texts*, 2004)	
Jp. Kōzengokokuron (興禪護國論)	2543
Eng. *A Treatise on Letting Zen Flourish to Protect the State* (in *Zen Texts*, 2005)	
Jp. Fukanzazengi (普勸坐禪儀)	2580
Eng. *A Universal Recommendation for True Zazen* (in *Zen Texts*, 2005)	
Jp. Shōbōgenzō (正法眼藏)	2582
Eng. *Shōbōgenzō: The True Dharma-eye Treasury* (Volume I, 2007) *Shōbōgenzō: The True Dharma-eye Treasury* (Volume II, 2008) *Shōbōgenzō: The True Dharma-eye Treasury* (Volume III, 2008) *Shōbōgenzō: The True Dharma-eye Treasury* (Volume IV, 2008)	
Jp. Zazenyōjinki (坐禪用心記)	2586
Eng. *Advice on the Practice of Zazen* (in *Zen Texts*, 2005)	
Jp. Senchakuhongannenbutsushū (選擇本願念佛集)	2608
Eng. *Senchaku Hongan Nembutsu Shū: A Collection of Passages on the Nembutsu Chosen in the Original Vow* (1997)	
Jp. Kenjōdoshinjitsukyōgyōshōmonrui (顯淨土眞實教行証文類)	2646
Eng. *Kyōgyōshinshō: On Teaching, Practice, Faith, and Enlightenment* (2003)	

Title	Taishō No.
Jp. Tannishō (歎異抄)	2661
Eng. *Tannishō: Passages Deploring Deviations of Faith* (1996)	
Jp. Rennyoshōninofumi (蓮如上人御文)	2668
Eng. *Rennyo Shōnin Ofumi: The Letters of Rennyo* (1996)	
Jp. Ōjōyōshū (往生要集)	2682
Jp. Risshōankokuron (立正安國論)	2688
Eng. *Risshōankokuron or The Treatise on the Establishment of the Orthodox Teaching and the Peace of the Nation* (in *Two Nichiren Texts,* 2003)	
Jp. Kaimokushō (開目抄)	2689
Eng. *Kaimokushō or Liberation from Blindness* (2000)	
Jp. Kanjinhonzonshō (觀心本尊抄)	2692
Eng. *Kanjinhonzonshō or The Most Venerable One Revealed by Introspecting Our Minds for the First Time at the Beginning of the Fifth of the Five Five Hundred-year Ages* (in *Two Nichiren Texts,* 2003)	
Ch. Fumuenzhongjing　(父母恩重經)	2887
Eng. *The Sutra on the Profundity of Filial Love* (in *Apocryphal Scriptures,* 2005)	
Jp. Hasshūkōyō (八宗綱要)	extracanonical
Eng. *The Essentials of the Eight Traditions* (1994)	
Jp. Sangōshīki (三教指帰)	extracanonical
Jp. Mappōtōmyōki (末法燈明記)	extracanonical
Eng. *The Candle of the Latter Dharma* (1994)	
Jp. Jūshichijōkenpō (十七條憲法)	extracanonical